TURN

WHAT IF FRESH AND FORCEFUL EXPRESSIONS OF THE CHURCH WERE RAISED UP TO TRANSFORM THE WORLD?

DR. ED LOVE

"But to those first in Damascus, and Jerusalem, and to all the country of Judea, and to the nations, I made known the command to repent and to turn to God, doing works worthy of repentance."
(Act 26:20)

Reflective Press

Copyright

Turn

Printed in the United States of America.

ISBN-13: 978-1466417786

ISBN-10: 1466417781

Cover and layout design by Reflective Design Company.

To every church planter who believes that Jesus is still the hope of the world...

WHAT OTHERS ARE SAYING

"Many authors hypothesize. Most consultants strategize. Ed and Phil understand the theories and know the best practices. They've done their homework but, more importantly, they've done the hard work. This is not an ivory tower treatise. This is a field manual written in the trenches of church planting. The Nitrogen Network is as close as I've ever been to the New Testament experience of a team of leaders and churches caring more about the mission than about their own survival. That's the essential fuel for a movement of multiplication. Don't just read this book. Allow it to stretch your faith and expand your vision for what is possible."

Dr. Mark Gorveatte, President of Kingswood University

"I have personally witnessed the transformation of many individuals and families who have connected into one of the Nitrogen Network churches. As a result of the movement, many lives are now moving toward being fully devoted to Christ. What Ed communicates so clearly is how God has and will continue to use ordinary people to bring others to Him."

Cindy Wessel, Regional Account Manager – Fleetwood Group

"It's been my joy to have a front-row seat as the Nitrogen Network has catalyzed a church multiplication movement. TURN gives its readers the opportunity peer into what God is doing and more importantly, join in it!"

Dr. Wayne Schmidt, Vice President of Wesley Seminary

"Your life...all of it...was meant to matter...for eternity. You have incredible God-given strengths and talents. They were given to you so that you could engage in the *turn*-around story of all time. Nothing fills our souls like joining God in His rescue of others... nothing. *Turn* is a first-rate roadmap for how to effectively involve ourselves in the God-venture we were created to live. Dr. Ed Love isn't just a theorist about missional ideas. He's a practitioner. He's done it. He's *doing* it. Allow *Turn* to breathe life into your soul."

Chris Conrad, District Superintendent for the West Michigan District within the Wesleyan Church

"Anyone who's followed the Lord of the Harvest into His harvest fields to join Him in starting a new church or ministry venture knows that it takes *work*. It takes *heart* work—the kind the Holy Spirit does when He cleanses and fills us with holy love and His passion for lost people. It takes *knee* work—activating spiritual authority with intentional intercession. It takes *home* work—taking the time to listen to the longings and discern the needs of people and then develop ministry to bring Jesus to them. The leaders within the Nitrogen Network are seeing amazing results in the harvest because they are consistently and persistently doing their heart work, knee work and homework on behalf of lost people. I'm proud to call these leaders my friends and teammates. Ed Love has done a great job telling the ongoing Nitrogen story. The fact that this network is growing within an established denomination makes their story even more remarkable. Catch their spirit and passion... learn from and adapt their principles and practices... and then follow their example. The Lord of the Harvest is calling... and lost people are waiting for us to come!"

Dr. Tim Roehl, Director of Church Health and Multiplication within the Wesleyan Church

CONTENTS

FOREWORD
BY PHIL STRUCKMEYER

The best definition I have ever heard of a church is: A church is a kingdom outpost. In other words, churches are supposed to be places on earth where the kingdom of God reigns and overflows to the world around it offering grace, compassion, forgiveness, repair, reconciliation, hope, healing, freedom and liberation.

I like to think of the kingdom of God like cell phone coverage. In cell phone coverage the key is cell phone towers. The more towers the more coverage. The more coverage the more powerful is the reign of AT&T or Verizon or even Boost. In the kingdom of God the key is churches. The more churches the more "coverage." The more "coverage" the more powerful is the reign of God's kingdom.

Today in North America there is a radical need for the planting of new churches. More and more we are finding, on our continent, that the kingdom coverage is not keeping up with the amount of grace, compassion, forgiveness, repair, reconciliation, hope, healing, freedom and liberation that is needed. We ultimately have a coverage problem and ultimately the problem can only be resolved by new "towers"... I mean churches.

TURN is an intriguing book which gives a powerful account of the small stories that God is using to create a little more "coverage" in our world. This book describes the seven values being lived out by a network of new churches that have been planted over the last eight years in the West Michigan region. Impact was planted in 2003 through the ministry of Kentwood Community Church and the West Michigan District of the Wesleyan Church. Impact planted Epic in 2006 and Encounter in 2007. Epic planted Pathway in 2009. Impact planted Ignite in 2009. And in 2011, Impact, Epic, Encounter, Pathway and Ignite are all planting The Well, The Dwelling Place, a campus out of Impact and a new work overseas called the Karis Project. In total, there are now nine new kingdom towers which have risen up within the last eight years.

The collective story of these churches has become known as *Nitrogen*, which is an emerging network mobilizing planters, churches, districts and other networks to start church planting movements in North America and beyond.

As you read through TURN, I know you will enjoy Dr. Ed Love's story-telling-style, his biblical insights and the introduction of key theological themes to our story. I hope that your heart will be captured and that you will truly be challenged to think more deeply about becoming a part of initiating and developing new kingdom-towers in our world.

Phillip Struckmeyer
Nitrogen Network Catalyst and Impact Network Pastor

INTRODUCTION
IT'S TIME TO TURN

"In the end, it's not the years in your life that count. It's the life in your years."
(Abraham Lincoln)

One of the most common questions in our go-go-go world is, "What time is it?"

We tend to ask the time-question when we need to go somewhere or get something done.

"What time is it?" is also a very common question in many locker rooms before any big game. Often, as the team captain pulls everyone together for an adrenaline-pumping pregame moment, the captain will shout, "What time is it?" Then, as the excitement builds, the teammates will respond in unison with, "Game time!"

Sometimes, if a team is really trying to get energized, the team members will repeat this cyclical mantra multiple times. At the end of their bantering, they will let out a bellowing roar, begin jumping up and down, and then head out to the court or field with fire in their eyes.

Since the majority of athletic competitions are psychological in nature, "What time is it?" is a good question to pose. This question allows the players to clear their minds of all distractions and focus on what really matters.

In the same way that players need to hear "What time is it?" before the big game, the body of Christ also needs to hear this action-oriented question today.

However, Jesus' team is not about winning the seasonal title.

Jesus' team is playing for an eternal banner.

Throughout history, there have been many great awakenings where radical men and women realized that new bands of people must rise up with a burning desire to turn their eyes upon Jesus. These audacious individuals all realized that attempting to "change the church" was a seemingly impossible task. Some bold leaders started entirely new movements and some tried to reinvent their churches from within their existing structures. Regardless of their path, all of these leaders understood the call from their Master to not just make a difference in the world, but to make a different world.

In relatively recent church history, there have been many new movements which have attempted to spruce up the church. Yet these fads and facades have quickly come and gone. Church leaders are now realizing that we need much more than fresh paint and creative arts in order to truly turn the church around. Church practitioners are discovering that we need deeply-committed-culturally-rebellious disciples of Jesus to rise up and roar, "It's game time!"

Despite the occasional glimmer of a budding mega/multi-site church, most of the American church stats are pretty bleak, to say the least.

Here are a few of the recent trends:

> It is estimated that nearly one million people a year are leaving the church in America.[1]
>
> 18% of Americans attend a church on any given Sunday.[2]
>
> 23% of Americans "regularly" attend a church (which is defined as attending at least 3 out of every 8 Sundays).[3]
>
> 37% of Americans "actively" attend a church (which is defined as 1 out of every 4 Sundays).[4]
>
> 52% of Americans "inactively" identify with a church.[5]
>
> 90% of all churches are plateaued or declining, 9% are growing because of church switching, and only 1% are growing because of true evangelism."[6]

Without a doubt times-have-changed, but have we forgotten that the church's responsibility in every age has always been to change-the-times?

You see, the church was given to the world precisely because God wanted to *turn* lives back to Him.

It may be true that church attendance is on the decline and approximately 3,500-4,500 churches are closing their doors each year.[7] But we must be careful not to ask the question, "How do we fix the church?" The church doesn't need fixing. The church that Jesus is leading is just fine.

What needs fixing is the world.

The church-question which will turn this world upside down is not, "How do we get more people in here?" The question that will revolutionize our society is, "How do we get more people on mission out there?"

The mission-oriented question isn't a new question. In fact, it's the same question Jesus was asking his followers in the first century.

On one occasion, Jesus said to his disciples, "The harvest is plentiful, but the workers are few. Ask the Lord of the harvest, therefore, to send out workers into his harvest field."[8]

Jesus knew that simply inviting people into a programmatic experience of worship, videos and teaching wasn't enough to truly turn their hearts and heads.

Jesus knew that true interior change would only come when a person accepted the challenge to *go*.

Even though the recent church trends reveal that the general populace is no longer interested in coming to well-crafted church experiences, the real problem in the church today is not an attendance problem—it's a going problem.

The stats on the American church may cause some to lose heart, but I'm certainly not living without hope. In many ways, the changing church landscape is helping the true church return to its axis.

I have the wonderful opportunity to meet and interact with many bold leaders who are attempting to hold fast to the core of our ancient faith and turn this world around.

From my vantage point, there is no doubt that God is raising up a new generation who is willing to carry out the old work order that Jesus gave his disciples:

> Therefore, *go* make disciples of all the nations, baptizing them in the name of the Father, the Son, and the Holy Spirit. Teach these new disciples to obey all the commands I have given you. And be sure of this: I am with you always, even to the end of the age.[9]

Jesus' G.O. (The Great Order) is still happening all across the globe in all kinds of forms and structures. It's interesting to note that Jesus never told his disciples "how" to go about fulfilling his G.O.—he simply promised to always be with us as we figured it out. For Jesus, the forms and functions were not a significant concern. He simply wanted the mission to be accomplished one way or another.

Even though there are thousands of groups all across the globe doing a phenomenal job at restoring the church, within this book we want to zoom in on one particular network where God is unmistakably turning a region around.

This book is an attempt to share the story, the stories and the ideology of one particular band of Christ followers. On one level, the movement in this network is nothing special—it's the same work of the Holy Spirit which was birthed on the day of Pentecost and emphasized throughout almost 2,000 years of church history. However, on another level, this network has some distinct qualities which may serve as a catalyst for other works of the Holy Spirit within the 21st century.

What makes this particular network unique is not that it is made up of many highly talented individuals—it's unique because it is made up of pretty ordinary individuals who simply want to love God with all of their heart, soul, strength and mind. And love their neighbors like they love themselves.[10]

Throughout my ministry experience, I have discovered that God can use anyone and practically anything to accomplish His eternal purposes. However, the stories that warm my heart the most are when I hear about someone who, by the world's standards, should not be able to accomplish very much.

For some reason, God enjoys using the weak to lead the strong.[11]

I love the story in Acts 4:13-14 where the people saw the courage of Peter and John and realized that they were simply unschooled, ordinary men. Nevertheless, they took note that Peter and John had been with Jesus.

If you were to spend some time with our network of church planters and pastors, you would quickly discover that it is merely a group of Jesus lovin' Peter and Johns. We are a rapidly multiplying cluster of unschooled, ordinary people, who love spending time with Jesus and have responded to God's question—"What time is it?"—with "It's game time!"

I have had the privilege to be a part of the network, which we now call *Nitrogen*, for the past six years. Over the years, I have watched God work in many awe-inspiring ways. I have watched old churches plant new churches, and new churches plant newer churches.

Witnessing the catalytic growth of these new churches is fun and exhilarating; however, the real joy that stems from our network is the fresh stories of life transformation.

It wasn't that long ago that some great friends of mine, Dean and Angela, were sitting on the sidelines watching the game-of-life pass them by. The stirring of a new church community in the area caused Angela to long for the God-relationship of her childhood. Dean, on the other hand, was pretty skeptical of any church event.

Nevertheless, he came.

And now he's going.

Dean and Angela recently moved to a nearby town and they are preparing to be a part of a new work of God in Ionia, MI, which is referred to as *The Well*.

The story of Dean and Angela is a special one. As a result of their newfound relationship with God, through Jesus

Christ, they will continue to be married. They will raise their kids to know, love and serve God. They will follow Jesus wherever he leads. And they are becoming less selfish and more and more Christ-like every day.

This network isn't about planting new churches.

This network is about the Deans and Angelas of the world.

I hope that this book will do two things in your life. First, I hope that you will see how God could use you (the good, the bad, and the ugly), to bring the light of Christ to the world around you. And secondly, I hope that this book will help shape your theology and churchology in a way that sparks a desire in you to participate in the broader movement of churches that are playing the only game that matters in life.

As a result of this book, maybe God will call you to be a part of a new church start in your community. Maybe God will call you to go into another city. Maybe God will call you to join in on the *Nitrogen* party. Or, maybe God will call you to start a new network of churches in your corner of the world.

Whatever it is, may God get the glory.

This is our story.

This is our song.

Praising our Savior, all the day long.

TURN

THE.WELL

EPIC

THE.KARIS.PROJECT

IGNITE

IMPACT

ENCOUNTER

PATHWAY

THE.DWELLING.PLACE

STAGE 1
TOWARD A MOVEMENT

"Never confuse movement with action."
(Ernest Hemingway)

"While they were worshiping the Lord and fasting, the Holy Spirit said, 'Set apart for me Barnabas and Saul for the work to which I have called them.' So after they had fasted and prayed, they placed their hands on them and sent them off."
(Acts 13:2-3)

From time to time I happen to come across people who are in need of car assistance. I always feel sorry for the person whose car happens to stall out in the middle of a busy intersection. Most of the time, I'll pull over, jump out and help push the car over to the shoulder.

On one occasion, I came across a lady who I could tell was quite frustrated with her vehicle. I jumped out of my truck, ran over to her and told her that I'd try to push her car out of the way. Now, there was a day when I could push cars by myself without any problem. However, after three kids and a busy life, I have become a little fluffy. I gave it my best though and after a lot of straining, groaning and sweating, I eventually pushed the car off to the side.

On another occasion, I again came across a lady who was stalled out at the corner of an intersection. I jumped out, ran over to the lady and told her that I'd try to push her car out of the turn lane. As I began to push, out of nowhere, another group of guys came running up and started pushing the car with me. After the guys-from-nowhere started to push, it almost felt like I wasn't even doing anything. The car picked up so much momentum that we had to yell at the lady to hit the brakes!

Pushing cars is much easier when you do it with others.

And so is the movement of God.

Wouldn't it be incredible if every local church body in every community was willing to see the world's needs, join forces and start pushing together?

What if churches didn't try to bind up their people, but truly encouraged and released them into whatever mission field God was leading them to be a part of?

Maybe, just maybe, the movement of God might start expanding like Wi-Fi.

There are several points throughout church history that we might point back to as "movement worthy." I must note, movement-worthy time periods are few and far between. But from the small number of movements that we can observe, there are several notable characteristics which help us see how God tends to work.

First, *a movement calls people to a seemingly impossible vision.*

In Mark 1:16-17 we read about the first two disciples that Jesus called into his life-altering movement. Jesus saw two fishermen, Simon and Andrew, who happened to be casting a net into the lake when Jesus was passing through. As the story goes, Jesus saw them and called out saying, "Come, follow me, and I will make you fishers of people."

Jesus' call was not only a call to action, but it was also a call to a seemingly impossible task. In the first century, the process of fishing was very different from today. Fishing with modern technology is hard enough, but imagine trying to fish with a couple of row boats and a net.

The text informs us that Simon and Andrew were practicing a technique called "cast-net fishing." Cast-net fishing could be accomplished in two ways. The first way was when one person would stand on the shore with one end of a very long net. The other end of the net would be attached to a boat. The people in the boat would push out away from the shore, make a large swooping circle, and eventually come back to the shoreline. The hope was that the large swooping action would capture all of the fish within the net's reach.

The second way to cast-net fish was by using two boats in the middle of the lake. Instead of one person situated on the shore, both boats would have one end of the net and together they would make a large circle hoping to capture all of the fish within that particular area. Since there was another fishing boat with Simon and Andrew's (James and John's), it's likely that they were using both of their boats to catch fish.

As you can imagine, cast-net fishing was not an easy task, and fishing was very labor intensive and an extremely tiresome job. It was very common for fishermen within the first century to go all day without catching a single fish.

Simon and Andrew would have known firsthand that Jesus' call to fish for people was essentially a call to the seemingly impossible. Nevertheless, the text says that they dropped their nets immediately and followed Jesus.

You see, Spirit-filled movements do not begin with cautious leaders.

Spirit filled movements begin with the brave and valiant.

One beautiful leadership story which has arisen out of our *Nitrogen Network* is the legend of Jim Bowen.

Jim was formerly the CEO of Impact Construction Homes and he basically had his entire life framed out. Jim had a good job, a house, a wife and two kids. Everything was fine without God—so he thought. One day as he was doing business as usual with a local lumberyard, he noticed that there was another business in the community which had the same name as his construction company. Jim's interest was peaked to say the least and it wasn't a positive vibe. Jim soon learned that the "business" was a new church in Lowell, MI, called *Impact*.

Just for clarity: *Impact Church* was initiated by the ministry of Kentwood Community Church and Phil Struckmeyer had been called to lead the charge.

Over time, Jim's curiosity in this new church got the best of him and he convinced his wife and kids to engage in the budding ministry of Impact. It wasn't long until a desire was placed in Jim's heart to respond to the good news of Jesus and lend a hand in the missional task. Jim put his construction background to use and started leading Impact's building and grounds crew.

However, swinging hammers and pounding nails for God was not the only desire stirring in Jim's heart. For some reason, Jim found himself longing to understand God's Word more and more, and he wanted to help others experience the salvific grace of God too.

Jim also began a discipleship path which eventually catapulted him into the student ministries of Impact. One day, Phil posed a question to Jim which forever changed his life. Phil asked Jim, "What would you think about joining our ministry team and becoming the leader of our youth ministry?"

Jim said, "I don't really know what I'm doing, but I'll give it a shot!"

Eventually, Jim was so overwhelmed by the impossible call that he decided to give up his lucrative construction business and serve God with 100% of his time.

Never in a million years did Jim (or his wife) envision "ministry" being a part of their life plan.

But God did.

Over the years, God grew Jim into a man of integrity, a man of the Word and a man of prayer. God also began to stir a desire in Jim to bring the good news of Jesus to the nearby community of Belding, MI. Jim encountered the living Jesus and he wanted everyone in his circle of influence to encounter him as well. So, Jim started a new discipleship band in Belding which in time formed Encounter Community Church.

The community of Belding is situated within a broken and depressed area of MI. Nevertheless, the movement of God was miraculously coming alive.

For three years, Jim led with passion, conviction and courage, and he even built up another strong leader named Rob Lawrence. In time, Jim eventually asked Rob to lead Encounter as he accepted another impossible task to reach the missing of Westland, MI (an eclectic suburb of Detroit).

In 2011, Encounter's leadership team installed Rob as the lead pastor and sent Jim out with love, respect and financial support.

The mission of God is now underway in Westland, and there is no doubt in anyone's mind that God will use Jim and his family as he calls others to another impossible task.

This is the legend of Jim Bowen; however, it is really no legend at all—it is entirely true. Jim's story is an incredible testimony of how God uses ordinary individuals to accomplish the extraordinary.

The second characteristic of a movement is that *the participants are not concerned as to who gets the kingdom credit.*

In Mark 10:35-45 there is an interesting story about two disciples who wanted to make a name for themselves. Mark describes the narrative in this way:

> Then James and John, the sons of Zebedee, came over and spoke to him. "Teacher," they said, "we want you to do us a favor." "What is your request?" he asked. They replied, "When you sit on your glorious throne, we want to sit in places of honor next to you, one on your right and the other on your left."
>
> But Jesus said to them, "You don't know what you are asking! Are you able to drink from the bitter cup of suffering I am about to drink? Are you able to be baptized with the baptism of suffering I must be baptized with?"
>
> "Oh yes," they replied, "we are able!"
>
> Then Jesus told them, "You will indeed drink from my bitter cup and be baptized with my baptism of suffering. But I have no right to say who will sit on my right or my left. God has prepared those places for the ones he has chosen."
>
> When the ten other disciples heard what James and John had asked, they were indignant. So Jesus called them together and said, "You know

> that the rulers in this world lord it over their people, and officials flaunt their authority over those under them. But among you it will be different. Whoever wants to be a leader among you must be your servant, and whoever wants to be first among you must be the slave of everyone else. For even the Son of Man came not to be served but to serve others and to give his life as a ransom for many." (NLT)

Now, before we shake our heads at James and John, we must realize that a little James and John are in each of us. We all suffer from what I refer to as the "aweso[me]-syndrome." We all have a tendency to think that God chose us because we are so spectacular. However, Jesus is quick to point out the fact that his disciples are to have a radically humble vantage point on life.

Furthermore, Mark makes an interesting comment within the narrative. Mark 10:41 points out that the ten other disciples heard what James and John had requested and they became indignant or annoyed.

You see, self-serving ministries do not create movements. People around self-serving churches tend to become put off and resentful. However, kingdom minded, sacrificial churches cause other churches, even churches outside of their network, to nod their heads and smile.

When people hear about another church giving "their" money, resources, time and talent away to another local church or church plant, they respond with awe and celebration.

The kingdom of God knows no denominational, hierarchical or religious boundaries. The kingdom of God is heaven on earth, and in this earthly expression of heaven, there are no church tribes, no church labels and no church logos.

The church is one people worshipping one Lord.

One of the exceptional unity-minded stories which arose out of the *Nitrogen Network* is a church community that goes by the name Ignite.

Ignite was Impact's third church plant project which began in 2009 under the leadership of Jim Nora. Every church plant is unique, but the distinct feature of Ignite is that it was also planted within Lowell, MI (which is the same town that Impact is rooted within). Bear in mind, Lowell is certainly not a high populace metropolitan suburb. However, in Phil Struckmeyer's mind, if the good news of Jesus was going to reach *all* people, then Lowell needed another fresh expression of the church.

Even though the body of Impact was experiencing great kingdom growth and fruit, God was at work, calling out people within Impact to go into their community and create another body which had the potential to reach more lives for Christ.

The leadership team of Impact could have easily said, "We'll just add another service and try to reach more people through another venue." Simply adding another service option was certainly a worthy idea; however, the Spirit was calling Phil to catalyze another entirely unique band of Christ followers who had a desire to reach the missing.

In the process of developing the new band of Christ followers in Lowell, God was in the process of calling Jim Nora to change vocations. Jim had a steady job with a local school district, but he heard and responded to the voice of the Lord calling him to pursue a life of leadership and ministry.

Jim's love for the Word and his heart for broken people are simply irresistible. Jim still works for his school district part-time, but he also works full-time for the Lord. Since the new church ignited in Lowell, several hundred people have been impacted by the ministry.

In addition to more lives in Lowell being changed and another missional outpost being initiated, the people of Impact have also been touched and humbled by the new ministry in their town. Because of Ignite's birth, more people in Lowell have been called into the movement—a movement where no one is concerned about the credit.

The third characteristic of a movement is that *it is entirely dependent upon God.*

In Luke 9:23-25 Jesus said, "Whoever wants to be my disciple must deny themselves and take up their cross daily and follow me. For whoever wants to save their life will lose it, but whoever loses their life for me will save it. What good is it for someone to gain the whole world, and yet lose or forfeit their very self?"

Here Jesus lays down the conditions of service for those who would follow him.

It becomes clear that Jesus did not want to collect a herd of Facebook fans—he wanted to collect radical disciples who would completely abandon the securities of the world. Once a person is stripped of all their securities, then, and only then, can they discover what it means to be entirely reliant upon God the Father.

Jesus' first condition was to "deny your-self."

To deny ourselves is to say, "I do not know myself." It is to ignore the very existence of oneself. Usually we treat ourselves as if we are the most important entity in the world; however, Jesus calls us to forget that we even exist.

This sense of personal denial was not meant to belittle an individual; it was intended to cause an individual to see beyond their I-centered ways and find out how to experience God's U-driven life.

Jesus' second condition was that his disciples were supposed to take up their cross (or their execution beam).

Jesus knew what crucifixion was long before he experienced it himself. In the first century, since the Roman authorities were not a very tolerant group of people, Roman vengeance was swift and sudden. Crucifixion was thought to be one of the best forms of execution precisely because the public spectacle warned others to not rebel.

To take up our cross means to be prepared to face hardship and suffering and still remain loyal to Jesus. It means to be ready to endure the worst of situations and still remain faithful to Christ.

Jesus' third condition was that his disciples must not be hoarders, but they must spend their life.

In the way of Jesus, the questions are not, "How much can *I get*?" but, "How much can *I give*?" Not, "What is the safe thing to do?" but, "What is the right thing to do?" Not, "What is the minimum work load?" but, "What is the maximum that I could offer to the cause of Christ?" As followers of Christ, we must realize that we were given life, not to keep for ourselves, but to spend it for others.[12]

Martin Luther had it right when he said, "What you do in your house is worth as much as if you did it up in heaven for our Lord God. We should accustom ourselves to think of our position and work as sacred and well-pleasing to God, not on account of the position and work, but on account of the word and faith from which the obedience and the work flow."

One individual within the *Nitrogen Network* who models Luke 9:23 in a significant way is Rob Lawrence. Rob is currently the leader of Encounter Community Church in Belding, MI (the church that Jim Bowen initiated). Rob came into the *Nitrogen Network* by way of transfusion.

Rob grew up in the central Michigan region and he had formerly led many different ministry adventures. Rob is an excellent leader and communicator. If truth be told, Rob could probably go on staff at any large church and he would do quite well. To this day, I'm still not sure why Rob chose to enter the *Nitrogen* circle-of-trust, but I'm very thankful that he did.

Rob had many other well-paying "ministry offers" to entertain; however, Rob's heart began to break for the missing and confused souls of Belding. Rob formed a relationship with Jim Bowen and they began co-pastoring Encounter. Over time, it was becoming clear that Rob was supposed to be the leader of Encounter and Jim was supposed to be sent out in order to plant another missional work. In May of 2011, the transition occurred and the movement multiplied.

Rob is an impeccable example of a disciple who is willing to deny himself, pick up his cross and follow Christ daily.

It would have been much easier for Rob to take the guaranteed salary package that other ministries were willing to provide, but Rob chose to lead a new body of believers further into the Way.

In the process of denying himself, it is evident that Rob has experienced complete dependency upon God. There are weeks that Rob doesn't know if he is going to receive his financial support, but he is persevering, nevertheless.

As a result of Rob's willingness to live dependent upon God alone, something unique is also happening within the body of Encounter. People are seeing Rob's example and they are beginning to toss their earthly crutches to the side and lean entirely on Christ for the first time. This movement toward dependency is actually bringing more and more stability to Encounter.

When we say, "God is at work" in a church, what we are really saying is, "God's people are becoming more and more dependent upon Him." Contrary to child rearing, dependency, not independency, is the goal. As the biblical narrative points out quite well, God works best when His people strive to be dependent on Him alone.

God enjoys saying to us, "My grace is sufficient for you, for my power is made perfect in weakness."[13]

And God blesses us when we say, "Therefore I will boast all the more gladly about my weaknesses, so that Christ's power may rest on me. That is why, for Christ's sake, I delight in weaknesses, in insults, in hardships, in persecutions, in difficulties. For when I am weak, then I am strong."[14]

In addition to the three movement-minded values, a movement also has three major structural components to take into consideration. In a unique way, all three components are evident within the *Nitrogen Network*.

The first structural component is the ability of the network to be *decentralized*.

In other words, things don't just happen within one place or around one leader.

Decentralization is a big word which basically describes how a large and complicated business or organization can become smaller and smaller. In decentralized theory, leaders of an organization will delegate the decision-making authority to the lower levels in the organization.

Decentralization moves away from a central authority, but it also moves toward a wider span of care. In the *Nitrogen Network*, there are some general pre-set guidelines but, for the most part, each local leader is allowed the opportunity to let the Spirit shape their local community how he or she sees fit. No leader in the network feels pigeon-holed into doing church in a certain style or way.

The advantage of being a part of a decentralized planting network is that each individual leader can truly respond to the voice of the Spirit. In the book of Acts, we read story after story where the early Apostles really were listening to the Spirit in surround-sound. The Apostles would respond to some of the most random ideas, but as the story progresses it becomes clear that God did have a plan all along.

In the *Nitrogen Network*, each church has the ability to plant new churches anywhere the Spirit calls them to go. We can plant a church in a rural context or an urban context. We can send out church planters from our churches and their new environments can look and feel completely different (and we celebrate this difference!).

No two network churches are the same, but we are all following the same Lord.

This reality leads into the second structural component of a movement which is: *segmentation*.

Decentralization concerns the decision making processes within an organization, but segmentation is what allows each church community to look different yet share similar values.

In biology, there is a process called *morphogenesis*. *Morphe* is Greek for "shape or transform," and *genesis* means creation. Literally, *morphogenesis* means, "The beginning of the transformation." Biologists refer to *morphogenesis* in reference to cellular growth and differentiation. It's interesting to note that *morphogenesis* can refer to different points in the cell's life cycle; it can refer to a mature organism or the embryonic stage.

In the same way that a cell lives in the constant ability to "begin the transformation," every individual church community also has the ability to multiply in fresh ways.

One great example of segmentation at work is what is happening at Impact under the leadership of Jason Holdridge (who is currently the lead pastor of Impact). Jason noticed that a large band of people were coming from the nearby community of Saranac and he felt compelled by the Spirit to launch a new work within Saranac. The heart behind this new campus is to take an already committed group of Christ followers and help them establish a new ministry within their area. This type of movement-mindedness is what keeps fresh works of the Spirit happening more often than not.

Segmentation allows each church within the *Nitrogen Network* to look and feel different, but each church has similar theological DNA. Each church might use different metaphors and vocabulary to define their mission, vision and values. However, they are all essentially saying the same thing in different ways. This sense of difference has allowed each individual planter to define the church environment according to their unique personality and what God places on their heart to flesh out.

Because of the network's ability to segment, we have found an increased sense of ownership across the board. We are also discovering that what connects in one community may not work in another community. Segmentation works for us, not against us. We can be as unique as we would like and still remain united.

This sense of unity draws us toward the third structural component of a movement which is: *interconnection*.

In telecommunications, interconnection is the physical linking of two networks for the mutual exchange of traffic. Under the Bell System Monopoly (1934), the Bell's owned the phones and did not allow interconnection, either of separate phones or other networks. Back then, a popular saying was, "Ma Bell has you by the calls!"

However, over time, the Bells realized that in order for telecommunications to advance, they would need to form interconnections.

"The mutual exchange of traffic" is a great way to describe our monthly *Nitrogen* huddles. Each month we band together for accountability, support, prayer, encouragement, equipping and strategizing. Without this sense of interconnection there is no doubt that our ability to spark a movement would be very limited.

Believe it or not, but most church leaders (even pastors within a denomination) feel very lonely.

Isolation is where the evil one works best.

There was a reason that Jesus said:

> Again, I tell you that if two of you on earth agree about anything you ask for, it will be done for you by my Father in heaven. For where two or three come together in my name, there am I with them.[15]

Here is one of these sayings of Jesus, whose meaning we need to probe a little deeper or we might miss the connection between our interconnections.

Jesus' *two or more* concern was not meant to be taken literally. Our heavenly Father certainly hears the cry of our hearts even when we are alone; however, Jesus was emphasizing another dynamic within his relationship with us.

First and foremost, Jesus' *two or more* insight means that prayer must never be selfish and that selfish prayer will not be answered. We are not only meant to pray only for our own needs and wants. We were meant to pray as members of one body, in agreement, remembering that life and the world are not arranged for us as individuals but for the body as a whole. More often than not, prayers for our “success” would necessarily involve someone else’s failure.

Can you imagine the family dynamics if a first child continually asked their father to pay for their tuition at Sarah Lawrence College in Bronxville, NY (the most expensive college in the U.S.), knowing that their father would not be able to support his other seven children in the same way? The first child’s request for success would leave his siblings drowning in resentment.

In the same way, Jesus wants to make sure that our prayers are not selfish prayers, and in order for our prayers to remain pure, we need other people around us as we pray.

Jesus goes on to say that *where two or three are gathered in his name, he is in the midst of them*.

In the first century, the Jews had a saying, “Where two sit and are occupied with the study of the Law, the glory of God is among them.”[16] Jesus essentially rephrases this ancient saying and inserted himself as the center of discussion.

Remember, Jesus came not to abolish the Old Testament law, but to fulfill it and be it.[17]

It is important to realize that church size does not determine the magnitude of the presence of God. Sometimes, modern USAmerican churches tend to glorify the numbers instead of glorifying Jesus. Jesus is just as much, if not more, present with a small band of disciples, than he is with the large crowd. Jesus is not a slave to numbers. Jesus is wherever faithful hearts meet, however few there may be.

Within our network huddles, we regularly experience the presence of Jesus. When we connect, either in a group or one on one, we know that Jesus is fully present. There is nothing more powerful than sitting on a grassy knoll in one of our towns crying, laughing, dreaming, strategizing and praying together.

There is an old saying that goes, "A family that prays together—stays together."

I think it can also be said, "A church planting network that prays together—stays together."

The question, "What if we were movement-minded?" is a question that every local church needs to answer.

Being a part of a movement is kind of like being a part of any family—it brings a few complications, but it also brings a lot of joy.

One thing is for sure, when a group of leaders band together in a decentralized, segregated and interconnected environment, God works miracles.

Questions to Consider

1. Do you feel like you are a part of a God-sized movement, why or why not?

2. Do you feel like you are living in a seemingly impossible God-given vision? If not, what is Jesus calling you to do?

3. How often do you find yourself encouraging, helping and praying for someone else's local ministry efforts?

4. What does it look like to be fully dependent upon God alone?

5. What are the advantages (or disadvantages) of orchestrating a decentralized, segmented and interconnected leadership environment?

STAGE 2
TOWARD THE KINGDOM OF GOD

"And so I am become a knight of the Kingdom of Dreams and Shadows!"
(Mark Twain)

"Jesus traveled through all the towns and villages of that area, teaching in the synagogues and announcing the Good News about the Kingdom. And he healed every kind of disease and illness."
(Matthew 9:35)

There is an old Anglican story of a man who felt compelled to visit a girl who was terminally ill. He wanted to bring the girl some cheer so he bought her a book that was designed to stir up a laugh. The man went to the girl's house, brought her a word of encouragement and then he gave her the book. The girl smiled and said, "I know of this book!" The man said, "Oh, have you already read it?" The girl responded, "Well, sort of—I wrote it!"

The kingdom of God is kind of like the girl's perspective on life. Jesus said himself that the kingdom he was ushering into the world would be filled with challenges; however, when viewed with the proper perspective, it is also a kingdom of immeasurable joy.

The difference between worldly happiness and Christian joy is that happiness is dependent upon consistent positive circumstances, while joy can be found within any situation—however bad it might be.

If truth be told, the work of the church is anything but glamorous. Even though church leaders do not usually show their true inner emotions, most leaders would concede that the pressure to lead a local church community is like standing in front of an active fire hydrant. Ministry is not easy, but for those who are convinced that God has called them to spray the good news of Jesus and equip the fire fighters, it is still incredibly rewarding.

Many times, church planters set out with grandiose visions, but they quickly discover that starting a new work is extremely complicated and a whole-lot-of-work! Sometimes, God moves in a community quickly, yet other times, because of resource challenges, facility oddities or relational fractures, it seems like it takes forever for the vision to unfold.

It's pretty typical that within the first two years of missional engagement, church planters reach a point where they discover the difference between building up their empire and being a part of God's kingdom.

You see, the majority of church planting is sowing the seeds.

One time the Apostle Paul stated, "And let us not grow weary of doing good, for in due season *we will reap*, if we do not give up."[18]

I worked on a farm as I was going through my Seminary experience. Before I personally experienced the farmer's life, for some reason, I thought that farmers had it made. I genuinely thought that all they had to do was throw out some seeds in the spring and then pick up the harvest in the fall. Cake job—right?

Far from it!

I quickly discovered that farmers work all year round and there is always something that needs to be done.

Now this is interesting: believe it or not, but the majority of farm work does not center on seeding or harvesting. The majority of the work is centered on *preparing* for the seeding and harvesting. Whether it's rigging up tractors, repairing equipment or buying supplies, there is always something to be done in the non-harvest seasons and it's usually quite urgent.

In the same way, church planting and disciple-making is a lot like farming. The majority of the labor is centered on the preparation aspects.

Steve Cymbal, one of our Nitrogen farmers, knows firsthand how challenging church planting can be. Even though the journey of planting a new church in St. Johns, MI, almost caused Steve's heart to give out, he is now giving-out-his-heart more than ever.

Steve planted the seeds of Pathway Church in 2009. Pathway is unique, in that, it is a grandchild of Impact Church. Just for clarity: Impact (2003) planted Epic (2006) and Epic planted Pathway (2009).

The reality is—Steve was given a hard assignment. Steve would describe the past few years as a bitter-sweet-symphony.

Epic provided Steve with some financial support and sent out a handful of people who had connections in St. Johns. The launch of Pathway was quite exhilarating and, by all church planting textbook standards, quite successful. Over 180 lives engaged in the early days, but those numbers faded out fairly quickly. After the launch-smoke dissipated, there were around 80-90 lives engaged.

Steve did a phenomenal job at cultivating his plant(s), but similar to farming, there are some things that simply cannot be controlled. Some years crops do very well and there is plenty of water; however, other years, there might be a drought in the region and the crops are found to be gnarly and withered.

Steve quickly realized that the culture's posture toward a new church is not, "Oh, we heard you are starting a new church and meeting in a school. That is so wonderful! Our community needs another church. I will bring my family every week without fail; we will serve and even give a tenth of our earnings to the new church. I'll be praying for you, daily!"

Not even close.

Like I said earlier, planting a new church is like farming—it's hard work.

Over the past two years, Steve began to realize that the hype of a new church launch cannot replace the intentional missional, incarnational and relational living which is necessary for true kingdom expansion.

In 2011, Steve reached a breaking point. The Spirit revealed to him that he had become a minister to people, instead of a minister of Christ. With the help of Epic and others in the network, Steve and his wife were allowed to get out of town for a couple of weeks and participate in a spiritual renewal retreat.

Steve is now a new man and he is leading a new kingdom centered ministry.

Steve is not only allowing the kingdom of God to grow in his own life, but he is also guiding the body of Pathway into a new season of missional impact. The Pathway body is now asking a different set of questions. Instead of asking, "How can we get people into our church?" they are asking, "How can we get into people's hearts within the St. Johns community?"

Steve is now taking these words of Jesus seriously: "They will see your good works and praise your Father in heaven."[19]

Miraculously, a new facility recently opened up to Pathway within the heart of St. Johns. Pathway is preparing for a new season of missional life. The church body is hoping that their facility will be an immense blessing to the community and that the kingdom of God will expand far beyond their church walls.

Steve is an incredible example of a spiritual farmer who wants to reach the missing and is willing to sacrifice short term success for long term kingdom fruit.

Steve sees the kingdom of God at work within the world and he is merely joining God in His labors.

Seeing the kingdom of God is certainly not an easy thing to identify. It seems like Jesus was constantly trying to show his disciples the kingdom that he was ushering in through his death and resurrection, but it took the disciples a long time to fully comprehend it. Most of Jesus' parables and image-based teachings dealt with seeing God's kingdom.

One time Jesus said,

> "The kingdom of God is like a farmer who planted good seed in his field. But that night as the workers slept, his enemy came and planted weeds among the wheat, then slipped away. When the crop began to grow and produced grain, the weeds also grew. The farmer's workers went to him and said, 'Sir, the field where you planted the good seed is full of weeds! Where did they come from?' 'An enemy has done this!' the

> Farmer exclaimed. 'Should we pull out the weeds?' they asked. 'No,' he replied, 'you'll uproot the wheat if you do. Let both grow until the harvest. Then I will tell the harvesters to sort out the weeds, tie them into bundles and burn them, and to put the wheat in the barn."[20]

Later, Jesus explained the parable to his disciples:

> "The Son of Man is the farmer who plants the good seed. The field is the world and the good seed represents the people of the kingdom. The weeds are the people who belong to the evil one. The enemy who planted the weeds among the wheat is the devil. The harvest is the end of the world, and the harvesters are the angels. Just as the weeds are sorted out and burned in the fire, so it will be at the end of the world. The Son of Man will send his angels, and they will remove from his kingdom everything that causes sin and all who do evil. And the angels will throw them into the fiery furnace, where there will be weeping and gnashing of teeth. Then the righteous will shine like the sun in their Father's kingdom. Anyone with ears to hear should listen and understand."[21]

The picture in this parable would have been clear and familiar to a Palestinian audience, because weeds were one of the primary curses against a farmer. The specific weed that Jesus would have been referring to in this parable was the *bearded darnel*. In the early stages of growth, the bearded darnel looks exactly like wheat.

Because of their similarities, by the time the plants were noticeably different, their roots had already intertwined, which made it impossible to pull up the bearded darnel without pulling up the wheat too.

Since both the bearded darnel and the wheat had to grow together, farmers were required to separate them during harvest season because the bearded darnel was poisonous in nature and could not be eaten.

To Jesus' hearers, this agrarian-parable was pretty self explanatory.

The kingdom-parable teaches us five things:

1) There is always a hostile power in the world, seeking and waiting to destroy the good seed.

2) It is hard to distinguish between those who are in the kingdom of God and those who are not.

3) We ought not judge people so quickly. If the farm-hands had their way, they would have torn out the bearded darnel and, as a result, they would have torn out the wheat as well.

4) The day of judgment for all humanity will come. It may seem like goodness never seems to be rewarded, but there will be a new world where everything is just and right.

And 5) The only person with the right to pass judgment is God. God is the only one who can discern the good and the bad.

Jesus' parable reminds us that what looks successful by human standards is often not successful before God. On one level, God's kingdom cannot be measured, calculated or manufactured; however, disciples of Jesus do know when they are *in* it.

Within the *Nitrogen Network*, we have two primary litmus test questions which help determine if our churches are *in* the kingdom of God.

The first litmus question is: *Do we fully understand the bigness of God*?

Someone once said, "The size of your worship is determined by the size of your God."

If we think that God is stuck in a box, then our faith will be the size of the box. The question isn't, "How big is your box?" the question is, "Do you have a box?" The kingdom of God is like the universe—it's all expansive and knows of no box.

In 1929 Edwin Hubble, working at the Carnegie Observatories in Pasadena, California, measured the redshifts of a number of distant galaxies. He also measured their relative distances by measuring the apparent brightness of a class of variable stars called Cepheids in each galaxy. When he plotted redshift against relative distance, he found that the redshift of distant galaxies increased as a linear function of their distance.

The only explanation for this observation is that the universe was still expanding.

Once scientists understood that the universe was expanding, they immediately realized that it would have been smaller in the past. At some point long-ago, the entire universe would have had a single beginning point. This means that the expanding universe is finite in both time and space.

The reason that the universe did not collapse, as Newton's and Einstein's equations said it might, is that it had been expanding from the moment of its creation. The universe is in a constant state of change. The expanding universe, a new idea based on modern physics, laid to rest the paradoxes that troubled astronomers from ancient times until the early 20th Century.

In the same way that the universe, God's created order, is always expanding, so it is with our relationship with God.

The expansiveness of God's creation is a reminder to us all that God's grace, love and forgiveness is unfathomable and immeasurable.

In Psalm 8, David's lyrics highlight the greatness of God:

> "LORD, our Lord, how majestic is your name in all the earth! You have set your glory in the heavens. Through the praise of children and infants you have established a stronghold against your enemies, to silence the foe and the avenger. When I consider your heavens, the work of your fingers, the moon and the stars, which you have

> set in place, what is mankind that you are mindful of them, human beings that you care for them? You have made them a little lower than the angels and crowned them with glory and honor. You made them rulers over the works of your hands; you put everything under their feet: all flocks and herds, and the animals of the wild, the birds in the sky, and the fish in the sea, all that swim the paths of the seas. LORD, our Lord, how majestic is your name in all the earth!"

God's invisible kingdom movement is just like God's all-expansive creation.

And when we see the bigness of God's kingdom, we can't help but be humbled and realize the shear smallness of our lives.

In 1885 a fellow by the name of Carl Boberg crafted a hymn which now goes by the name, "How Great Thou Art." The inspiration for the song came when Boberg and some friends were returning home to Mönsterås from Kronobäck, where they had participated in an afternoon church service. Nature was at its peak that radiant afternoon. A thunderstorm appeared on the horizon, and soon sharp lightning flashed across the sky. Strong winds swept over the meadows and billowing fields of grain. The thunder pealed in loud claps. Then rain came in cool fresh showers. In a little while the storm was over and a rainbow appeared.

When Boberg arrived home, he opened the window and saw the bay of Mönsterås like a mirror before him. From the woods on the other side of the bay, he heard the song of a bird and the church bells were tolling in the quiet evening. It was this series of sights, sounds and experiences that inspired the writing of *How Great Thou Art*.

According to Boberg's great-nephew, Bud Boberg, the origin of the song was a paraphrase of Psalm 8 and was used in the underground church in Sweden in the late 1800s when the Baptists and Mission Friends were persecuted.[22]

Within our network of churches, we all want to make sure that everyone is exposed to our limitless and infinite God.

When people see the greatness of God, they can't help but respond with action.

We like to say, "Our *inspiration* comes from the bigness of God, but our *perspiration* comes from the smallness of God."

This thought leads to our second kingdom litmus test question which is: *Do we fully understand the smallness of God?*

God is all-expansive, but He is also small enough to be woven into the very fabric of our lives. God's glory can be found in the mind-blowing galaxies, but it can also be found in giving a cup of cold water to a thirsty soul. God is in the small things of life, just as much as He is in the big things.

It's interesting to note that quantum mechanics has led many scientists to conclude that there must be a God who started everything.

Quantum mechanics was developed early in the twentieth century in an attempt to explain the seemingly random behavior of atoms (the smallest features of the world). The rules of classical physics didn't apply to atoms, so scientists set out to understand why atoms were so unpredictable.

Probability reigns supreme in quantum mechanics. And subatomic particles do not have definite properties for certain attributes such as position, momentum or direction of spin *until they are measured.* It's not that those qualities are unknown; it's that they do not exist in any definite state until they are measured. They behave as waves when not observed, but as particles in a definite location when observed. The position of the atom is thus an "observer-created reality."

Until observation, the atom is in a "superposition state." If you were to fire the atom toward two boxes, A and B, the box would simultaneously be in both box A *and* B until you looked to see where it was. Until you looked, you could not say it was in either box, you could only speak of *probabilities* that it would be found in one location or the other. But the electron does not have a definite location until it is observed.

Now it really gets wild. The observer can be human (conscious being) or a machine (like a Geiger counter). But the machine is a physical instrument and subject to the rules of quantum mechanics, so it too enters into a superposition state along with the atom. In other words, the results are suspended as it awaits being observed by a conscious being.

Physicist Von Neumann argued that, "The entire physical world is quantum mechanical, so the process that collapses the wave functions into actual facts cannot be a physical process; instead, the intervention of something from outside of physics is required. *Something nonphysical*, not subject to the laws of quantum mechanics, must account for the collapse of the wave function: the only nonphysical entity in the observation process that von Neumann could think of was the consciousness of the observer. He reluctantly concluded that this outside entity had to be consciousness and that prior to observation, even measuring instruments interacting with a quantum system must exist in an indefinite state."

Do you grasp what he's saying?

In the creation of this material world, something other than physical processes had to exist (A.K.A.—God).

Even more, simply by "observing" us, God is "sustaining" us.

God not only sees us, but He also designed the smallest microscopic atoms which sustain us. God's attention to detail is just as much unfathomable and immeasurable as God's all-expansive created order.

One time, Jesus captured the essence of the bigness and smallness of God's kingdom in a powerful image. In Mark 4:30-32 Jesus said,

> What shall we say the kingdom of God is like, or what parable shall we use to describe it? It is like a mustard seed, which is the smallest of all seeds on earth. Yet when planted, it grows and becomes the largest of all garden plants, with such big branches that the birds can perch in its shade.

Jesus knew that his kingdom was one of those concepts which would be difficult to understand. We can easily make sense of earthly kingdoms since they can be explained geographically with boundaries, and politically with a definable government. We can study the ancient kingdoms of Babylon and Egypt, and we can grasp their territories, monarchical governments and cultural control. But the kingdom of God is different. It has no boundaries geographically, spatially or in terms of its governance.

Ancient kingdoms regularly displayed their might through dazzling parades, magnificent buildings, extravagant celebrations and grandiose armies. Sometimes, the ancients would construct new roads and buildings in order to accommodate a solitary visit from the emperor or king. In a sense, people measured kingdoms by how large of a splash they could make in a given setting.

So when Jesus announced the arrival of the kingdom of God, the first century mind expected parades, armies, construction projects and a plan to expand the territory.

But pomp and prestige was the last thing on Jesus' mind.

The primary reason that Jesus' disciples struggled with the concept of God's kingdom was because it seemed rather insignificant and powerless.

The parable of the tiny mustard seed teaches us that the kingdom of God will always have small beginnings. It may appear insignificant and without influence, yet we can be certain of its pervasive growth. God's kingdom is not dependent upon the displays of human might. By sovereign design, the kingdom begins from the smallest of beginnings and grows into something that will be greater than anyone could have imagined from the outset.

For Jesus' disciples, with all that was going on in the Roman Empire during the first century, it may have felt like their missional seed was so insignificant. I'm sure they wondered if the unseen kingdom of God would make any difference in the world. But I think it is safe to say that God's kingdom has undoubtedly changed the world.

In our network churches we often speak about desiring to see lives changed. However, what we really mean is, we desire to see lives enter into the kingdom of God. Once a person acknowledges allegiance to the King of Kings and Lord of Lords, then and only then, can the values of the kingdom begin restoring and changing individual lives. In all of our communities, we are not trying to simply modify people's behavior—we are trying to help people learn how to submit to the world's true King.

You see, as a person submits to the King and adopts the kingdom's value system, everything begins to transform.

The seed begins to grow into a productive shade tree.

The process of transforming from a seed into a tree doesn't happen overnight. It's important to realize that the macro-kingdom growth we all desire only happens by micro-acts-of-service.

One time Jesus said to his disciples, "Instead, whoever wants to become great among you must be your servant, and whoever wants to be first must be your slave—just as the Son of Man did not come to be served, but to serve, and to give his life as a ransom for many."[23]

The world judges success by how big something feels, but Jesus wants to know, "How small are you becoming?"

In another teaching, Jesus also said, "Be faithful in the small things and you will be rewarded with the big things."[24]

If we want to see people experience greatness in life, then we need to show them how to live big in small ways.

I was recently reminded about the big impact of small acts of kingdom service when I was talking to a widow (who happens to be a part of the Epic body). A few years ago this woman's husband left her and she doesn't have any family around. So, when she speaks of her family, she speaks of her church. As we were talking, with a huge smile on her face, she shared with me how blessed she was when she was preparing to move. Duane Bower (Epic's current lead pastor) heard about her big move and called every Epic man to come and help this woman move.

Because of Duane's willingness to coordinate a small act of kindness, not only did the body of Epic move a life, but they also moved a soul.

In all of our network churches, we not only want to draw attention to the bigness of God, but we also want people to see how God is at work within the little things.

In our minds, kingdom-mindedness means that we must be mesmerized by the small.

How small can you get?

Questions to Consider

1. In your own words, how would you describe the kingdom of God?

2. How does the bigness of God affect your everyday life?

3. How does the smallness of God affect your everyday life?

4. In what ways does the kingdom of God work like a tiny mustard seed?

5. Over the past six months, how have you seen God use something small for His glory?

STAGE 3
TOWARD INCARNATIONAL LIVING

"God became what we are that He might make us what He is."
(Athanasius)

"As you go, preach this message: 'The kingdom of heaven is near.'"
(Jesus the Messiah)

One of my favorite shows is "The Undercover Boss." In the show, CEOs of major companies disband their fancy offices and join the labor force on the front lines of their business. As the bosses become bossed, there is a deep inner transformation which occurs. Not only does the boss realize their own weakness, but they also have the opportunity to peer into the hearts of those who work for them.

The incarnation is kind of like The Undercover Boss experience.

God comes from above in order to work from below.

The incarnation is the central miracle within every generation. Christians believe that God became man and this man dwelt among us.

The word *incarnation* literally means embodied in flesh or taking on flesh. Christianity is rooted in the process of God descending in order to re-ascend. In other words,

Jesus was God's salvific-seed planted into the dark and sinful soil of the world, with the expectation that the seed of God would rise again full of hope.

Without the incarnation, Christianity is just another nice religious option which promotes human politeness. However, with the incarnation, Christianity is a hope-filled movement worth sacrificing your life.

You see, the incarnation of Jesus causes God's people to do the same for the people around them.

In the letter to the church in Philippi, the Apostle Paul described the effect of the incarnation on humanity in this way:

> In your *relationships with one another*, have the same mindset as Christ Jesus:
>
> Who, being in very nature God, did not consider equality with God something to be used to his own advantage; rather, he made himself nothing by taking the very nature of a servant, being made in human likeness. And being found in appearance as a man, he humbled himself by becoming obedient to death—even death on a cross!
>
> Therefore God exalted him to the highest place and gave him the name that is above every name, that at the name of Jesus every knee should bow, in heaven and on earth and under the earth, and

every tongue acknowledge that Jesus Christ is Lord, to the glory of God the Father.[25]

It's interesting to note that Philippians 2:5-11 is presumably one of the first Christian creeds (which would have been sung, by the way).

Notice that the creed begins by saying, "In your *relationships with one another*, have the same mindset as Christ Jesus."

Immediately, we discover that Jesus' followers are called to be Jesus to the people around them. In other words, the Apostle Paul was calling God's people to *incarnate* themselves *into* the world in the same way that Jesus did.

Within our network churches, we often speak about "being" the church as opposed to just "going" to church. Simply "going to church" implies a passive state, where as "being the church" implies presence.

Recently, I was in the town of Ionia, where our most recent missional outpost is simmering. I was talking with someone from the community who had heard that we were starting a new church. Not surprisingly, her first question to me was, "Where are you at?" Even though I didn't say it, my first internal response was, "Right in front of you!" I knew the questioner was just trying to make small talk, so I politely shared that our small band of Christ followers were meeting in an old lumber yard on the east side of town.

The truth is; the majority of Americans (even the post-Christian segments) believe that church is a building where spiritually-oriented people attend an event and consume their spiritual-goods.

Honestly, it has taken me a long time and a lot of theological training in order to see the true church, the people of God, who are clothed in Jesus Christ.

As a young lad, I was trained in the church-is-a-building ideology. I remember being taught the old Sunday school gesture where you clasp your fingers together and say, "Here is the church, here is the steeple, open the doors, and look at all the people!" As kids we had a lot of fun with the steeple-producing gesture, but if I were able to rephrase the old saying today for my kids I would hold up all of my fingers and say, "Here are the people, there will never be a steeple, open the garage door and let in more people!"

I don't know if that gesture and phrase will ever catch on, but I wish it would!

In all of our network churches, which do happen to meet in some sort of facility, we try our best to craft new language which embraces our re-incarnated theological framework.

We want people to know that *Wii* are the church.

With that said, we also know that facilities can serve as functional ministry tools in our American culture. We might have to fight off the old "church as a building" way of thinking, but we have attempted to redefine our space. Instead of thinking of our facilities as "the place to be," we are trying to help people see that our facilities are "the place to leave."

The place to be is in people's lives.
The place to be is with the sinners and tax collectors.

I think it is important to keep in mind that if Jesus were to come and visit our church facilities today, he would not walk around saying, "You all have done an amazing job around here. This is state of the art!" Not at all. Jesus would come into our facilities and ask us, "So, what people groups are you sending people into? Who is spending time with the poor and marginalized? Who is taking care of the orphans? Who is mentoring the fatherless children? Who is repairing marriages? Who is digging wells in barren communities? Who is taking care of the widows?"

Jesus wants to know *who* is being *him* in the world.

Within our network churches, there are countless stories of people who understand that the church body comes to-gather in order to be scattered. One unique story is the tale of Michael Will (which arose out of Epic Church while I was the lead planter/pastor).

I first connected with Michael while he was in prison. Michael's mother heard about Epic when we were just beginning, and she told Michael that he should write me and see if there was anyone who would write him back from time to time. Michael found Jesus while he was in prison and he was beginning to see the reason for a church community. From what Michael had heard, Epic was apparently a "different" kind of church. In other words, his mother was thinking that Epic might actually be a place that Michael would be accepted and loved by others regardless of his past blemishes.

When I received Michael's first letter, the Spirit compelled me to continue writing him on an ongoing basis. I recalled that Jesus was recorded in the 25th chapter of Matthew as teaching that we should "visit" prisoners, and by extension, to be kind and merciful to them.

So, Michael and I became pen-pals.

It was clear that God was working in Michael's life and he wanted to know Jesus and make him known. After a year and half of writing, Michael was released from prison and one of his first stops when he came home was to meet me in person. When we met, we embraced each other like old friends. We celebrated his release and started talking about what God was up to in the Portland region. Michael jumped in right away and started serving at Epic. Two weeks after he was released from prison, we gave him a key to our facility (which we laugh about now). He really did think we were crazy for giving a parolee the key to our facility.

The truth is—we were crazy, but we were crazy about fresh acts of the church. When we began Epic, our desire was to reach the missing at whatever cost. We did not want to see a bunch of previously churched people swapping their membership for something new and improved. We genuinely wanted to run after the one lost sheep. If people needed a church home, then they were certainly free to join us. But our attention was not on the ninety nine.

Our attention was on the one lost sheep.

Michael is now working toward a substance abuse counselling degree and pursuing ministerial training. He also started a new ministry called 180, which is designed to provide healing and reconciliation for people who struggle with all sorts of addictions.

Simply put, Michael is a fresh expression of the church.

Another fresh expression of a re-incarnated church comes out of Encounter's ministry. As Jim Bowen was initiating the new work in Belding, he realized that one of the holes in the community happened to be single moms, young parents and expecting mothers. Many times, these individuals are left struggling and alone. In order to help fill the community need, the Encounter team came up with the brilliant idea to fund and staff, what they call, the Cares Ministry.

The Cares Ministry focuses on helping anyone who is struggling to care for a young child. The body of Encounter provides many essential items, such as, diapers (lots of them), wipes, formula, baby food, gas drops, bottles and inserts, pacifiers, baby wash and shampoo, laundry soap, ointments, clothing and even baby furniture.

Another aspect of the Cares Ministry, which is located in a downtown shopping complex, is that the leaders have strategically attempted to build bridges into the community's business district. Many businesses are now participating and engaging in Encounter's ministry.

The Cares Ministry is one of many examples which are attempting to provide the world with fresh expressions and acts of the church. Many of these new expressions do have social justice components involved; however, our network churches want it to be clear that as we come in the flesh to meet tangible needs within our world, we are also strategically leading people into the way of Jesus. For us, meeting community needs and proclaiming the good news of Jesus go hand in hand.

One incredible account that arose out of Encounter's Cares Ministry was the story of Marcy. Marcy connected into the body of Encounter as the result of a tragedy. Marcy happened to be driving behind a man named Jeff Wittung, who was very involved in Encounter's ministry, when his vehicle collided head on with another vehicle. Sadly, Jeff passed away from the crash injuries. Marcy did not know Jeff at the time, but in her healing process, she came to know Jeff's wife, Marne. As you can imagine, the journey for Marne has not been an easy one; however, she has watched God use the tragedy for His good purposes.

Marne quickly developed a relationship with Marcy. Marne invited Marcy to come to a few Encounter gatherings. Most of what Marcy experienced at Encounter was new and news to her. She was beginning to connect. And, for some reason, Marcy was compelled to help out in Encounter's Cares Ministry. Eventually, Marcy was so overwhelmed by the impact of the Cares Ministry that she decided to become a co-leader of the ministry. Through the Cares Ministry, God was drawing near to Marcy. Yet it wasn't until September of 2011 that Marcy finally surrendered her life to Christ at Encounter's women's retreat.

Marcy's surrender-moment was a shock to everyone primarily because she was so involved with the Cares Ministry. People just assumed that she had a growing relationship with Christ. However, the entire time that Marcy was serving others, God was using those acts of kindness to soften Marcy's heart. Part of Marcy's testimony is that she saw Christ, not primarily through a church service, but through the selfless acts of those who served with her in the Cares Ministry. Now, Marcy and her husband are growing closer to the Lord every day and serving everyone they can.

Within the *Nitrogen Network*, stories like Marcy's cause us to continue doing what we are doing, even when it is not glamorous or glossy.

The real heroes of our churches are those who understand the personal implications of Jesus' incarnation.

A friend of mine named Dave VanKulen is also another great network example of an individual who wants to incarnate himself into our God-less world. Dave is connected to Impact and he is an incredible sound technician and musician. Dave's heart became broken for the musicians in his community and he came up with a beautiful idea called Sessions-at-Impact. SAI is an event where community bands can come in and use Impact's facilities to jam and record their music. Through SAI, Dave has had the opportunity to connect with many artists who probably would not connect to the church otherwise.

Dave has realized that in order for the church to rise up, we must begin thinking creatively as to how we can be like Jesus—coming from above and working from below.

When I was in grade school, my favorite days were when we would have show-and-tell event. I would usually bring in some random object from nature like a turkey feather, snail or turtle shell, but regardless of what it was, my classmates always seemed interested.

Stirring interest in others is part of the reason that God needed to send His one and only Son into our world. God was not only showing the world who He was, but He was also telling us how to truly live.

We have discovered that *incarnation* (the call to go into the world as Jesus' representatives) leads to *impartation* (the call to share the message of Jesus), which then leads to *in-listment* (the call to invite others in).

The world didn't just need another religious idea.

The world needed to see God in the flesh.

QUESTIONS TO CONSIDER

1. If a child came to you and asked you to describe the incarnation, how would you explain it?

2. How does the incarnation affect your relationships and attitudes?

3. Do you struggle with the church-is-a-place-you-go mindset? If so, why?

4. When was the last time that you felt like someone was being Jesus to you?

5. When was the last time you felt like you were being Jesus to someone else?

STAGE 4
TOWARD A REDEMPTIVE VISION

"God loves to hear from strangers."
(Dion Dimucci)

"Hope in the Lord; for with the Lord there is unfailing love. His redemption overflows."
(Psalm 130:7)

T.I. was facing 30 years in prison.

The Grammy-winning rapper was at the apex of his career but was about to lose it all because of a mistake earlier in his life.

However, as part of a deal worked out between his lawyers and the federal government, if he completed 1,000 hours of community service by March, that sentence could be reduced.

At 27, T.I. began seeking redemption and helping others avoid the mistakes that he made. In the M.T.V. series *T.I.'s Road to Redemption: 45 Days to Go* cameras followed T.I.'s efforts to save himself by saving others. In order to communicate his message, he had to give each teenager a tough love lesson in life and show them the consequences of what could happen if they continued down the wrong path.

The series followed T.I. as he talked to schools and community groups about how to avoid the trouble he fell into, but it also followed T.I.'s personal journey of seeking redemption.

In the end, the show was an incredible presentation of one man longing to make things right.

T.I. redeemed himself.

Our American culture may have a lot of problems, but, by and large, our society is pretty forgiving after a person walks through the redemption process.

Redemption is respectable when it is genuine.

One time, early on in our Portland church planting adventure, I had someone steal my guitar and many other items from within our facility. We knew that it was most likely an inside job, since our facility had been locked up tight.

It wasn't until three years later that we found out who stole our stuff. A gang of church thieves had finally gotten busted, and it came out into the open that they were the Epic thieves. Shockingly, one of the thieves was actually a part of Epic and I had personally mentored him. After this particular thief confessed everything to the police officers, I received a phone call stating that my guitar was down at the police station. I said, "You've got to be kidding!"

My guitar eventually found its way back to me.

And so did my thief.

The fellow who organized the Epic crime came to me broken and seeking redemption. He felt guilty and ashamed. After he asked for forgiveness, I said, “Forgiveness for what?” I let him know that I would never judge him or think differently about him because of what he did. The young man was fully restored to the body of Epic and is now growing in his relationship with God.

In the biblical narrative, redemption is described as the act of being delivered from sin or being saved from evil.

In our network churches, we strive to celebrate the genuine redemption stories. Each church community longs to see redeemed souls, redeemed addicts, redeemed finances, redeemed marriages and redeemed families.

The stories that we celebrate are not how many people attended our Easter gatherings, but they are the stories like Rob and Judy Smith (a family connected to Impact).

As a boy, Rob was abused. Out of his anger and confusion he turned to drugs and alcohol in order to escape from his problems. Rob eventually married Judy and they had three children together. However, marriage and children didn’t solve any of Rob’s inner problems. His life was one big roller coaster of ups and downs. After the final marital straw broke, he found himself separated and drinking his life away. One Saturday night he felt something tell him to connect at an Impact gathering. After the gathering he went up to Jason Holdridge (Impact’s lead pastor) and started weeping uncontrollably.

God was speaking and saving.

A few weeks later, Rob's wife, Judy, came to know Christ too. One night as Jason connected with their family over a meal, the entire family had a moment of collective redemption. They didn't know it, but God had been speaking to each one of them and calling them home. A few weeks later, Rob, Judy, and their daughter Shelby, were baptized. Now, the Smith family exists to serve God and serve others. Rob has initiated an incredible prison ministry and ministers to some of the most difficult individuals. Rob has been sober for two years, his marriage has been redeemed and he couldn't be more grateful.

Stories like Rob and Judy are happening all the time throughout our network churches. These stories fill our hearts with joy because we know that God is not dead. No. God is fully alive, at work within the world and the Lord's Prayer is being answered.

Our network churches take Jesus seriously when he prayed, "Our Father who is in heaven, hollowed be your name, your kingdom come, your will be done, *on earth* as it is in heaven." [26] Unless you are ready for significant life change, I wouldn't recommend praying Jesus' prayer. The Lord's Prayer can be a wonderful part of church liturgy; however, if you really take Jesus' theology seriously something radical must transpire.

Jesus really did envision heaven coming to earth. In fact, he told his disciples, not to pray to get into heaven, but to pray to get heaven into earth.

Honestly, the earthly reality of heaven is what caused me to reshape another community. If you will permit me, I'd like to share a little bit of my story with you.

Phil Struckmeyer and the Impact team was feeling compelled to plant their first church in 2005. Many communities were on their radar, but the town of Portland, MI, seemed to strike a missional chord. Phil contacted me to see if I would be interested in planting a new church in Portland. Emily, my then pregnant wife, and I said that we'd explore and look into the Portland opportunity. Within weeks the Lord confirmed the decision to move and begin the new work. We eventually scrounged up 12 rugged disciples who wanted to impact Portland with the good news of Jesus. With these 12 audacious souls, we planted Epic Church in 2006. The mission gripped and many people came to know the Lord.

In 2009, we were put into a position where we needed to make a decision about our facility situation. We had originally started collecting lives within an old crusty American Legion hall, but we soon discovered that the Legion fellows wanted to sell their space. Around that time, a strip-mall facility opened up to us and our community raised the necessary funds and renovated it to fit our needs.

We were in the new facility for about a year and the mission was going great. However, the Lord began to break my heart for more of the missing. I remember my calling clearly. I was in the last week of a teaching series called *Broken: Pursuing the Missing*. As I was giving the invitation for the body of Epic to go and reach the missing in their circle of influence, I received a call to go and reach the missing in the nearby community of Ionia. It was a very strange experience to say the least. I was being prompted by the Spirit to go as I was telling everyone else to go.

As you can imagine, leaving a church community that you planted and dearly love is not an easy thing to do. Good, bad, right or wrong, I held my Ionia calling to myself for a long period of time. If I am being honest, this call didn't make a lick of sense to me. I had just gotten the environment of Epic steady and then God had to go and call me to another initiative. Needless to say, I spent several months wrestling with God in regards to this new call. In fact, I even started exploring other communities to plant in, but God kept bringing me back to Ionia. Ionia isn't a well-to-do city. Actually, in planters lingo, Ionia would be considered very "hard soil."

Nevertheless, we shared the Ionia call with the body of Epic and we asked them to "kick us out." Now, at the same time my call was happening, we also had another person within Epic who was being called out and up too. Duane Bower had received a call to pursue a life of pastoral ministry in 2010. Duane had a great job working for the State of Michigan, but he was ready to step up to the challenge and had already proven himself in pastoral leadership. Duane had already started his ministerial education and he had experienced an internship at Epic.

Well, one Sunday morning, I was in the back listening to Duane speaking and the Spirit confirmed that Duane was ready to lead Epic into the future.

Tears saturated my eyes and I knew that Duane was being called and the movement of God was about to multiply once again.

The move toward Ionia was extremely unique. Approximately 12 individuals who were a part of Epic lived or worked in Ionia. At the same time God was calling me to go, God was also calling these other individuals too. Each family began to sense a Spirit-led desire to go *into* Ionia, instead of going away.

In August of 2011, we made the decision official and began working toward the development of a new hope-filled community called *The Well*. One of the disciples who God was calling also happened to own an old lumber yard which had an open floor plan. Since no one in our group had a house that was suitable for all of our children, we assumed that this building was God's provision. We began meeting, reading the Scriptures together and praying for the Lord to work in the area.

The Well is in the early phases of mission development, but lives are already being transformed by the gospel of Jesus. It is amazing what happens when a committed group of believers submit their lives to the Lord. We don't know what everything will look like, but we are certain that God has a plan to reach the missing.

God desperately wants to redeem the world.

And He wants to use us in the process.

QUESTIONS TO CONSIDER

1. How would you describe the word *redemption*?
2. Have you ever experienced redemption in your life? If so, how?
3. How does God's form of redemption differ from the world's form of redemption?
4. If Jesus brought heaven into earth, how does that reality change the way you live?
5. How does the planting of new churches affect God's redemptive vision in the world?

STAGE 5
TOWARD SACRIFICE AND GENEROSITY

"God has given us two hands—one to receive with and the other to give with. We are not cisterns made for hoarding; we are channels made for sharing."
(Billy Graham)

"In everything I did, I showed you that by this kind of hard work we must help the weak, remembering the words the Lord Jesus said: 'It is more blessed to give than to receive.' "
(Acts 20:35)

As it is with any great redemptive initiative in the world—it takes financial resources to sustain the movement.

Throughout the Scriptures, God was never found to be bashful when speaking about money matters. In fact, Jesus talked more about money than he did about any other subject, including heaven and hell combined.

Jesus knew that if there was one area in our lives which could ruin all of our lives, it was the area of money and possessions. Jesus knew that the almighty dollar has the power to negatively affect the important things in life, such as, a person's marriage, family and all other relationships.

The heart behind Jesus' teachings on money was not that God needed the money; it was that people needed to be free from the dollar's death claws.

On one occasion Jesus said, "Wherever your money is there your heart is as well."[27]

Another time, Jesus highlighted a poor woman who was giving her offering at the temple. The text says that the woman gave all that she had (which was the equivalent of two pennies). You see, Jesus wasn't concerned about the amount that she was giving—he was concerned about her heart. Jesus goes on and contrasts the woman's generous offering to the offerings of the wealthy religious leaders. The religious leaders were giving out of their abundance, but this woman was giving out of her poverty. The woman could have easily said, "These two pennies won't make much difference anyways, in fact, it would be better if I just kept them and bought some bread for a meal tonight." Yet she doesn't say that. She gave generously and sacrificially. She wanted her money to go to work in the kingdom of God.

It's easy to give out of our abundance and leftovers.

But spare giving doesn't catalyze a movement.

Spare giving will only maintain the status quo.
The truth is, we live in a world where we are constantly being bombarded with enticements to satisfy our selfish

desires, and the idea of giving at a level which is truly sacrificial is new territory for most people. It takes a major leap of faith to go from spare giving to sacrificial giving.

In the book of Acts we read about people who were willing to sell their land and bring the proceeds to the apostles so that they could distribute it toward kingdom purposes.

(Take a moment and picture that scene).

The heart behind that type of sacrificial giving is certainly a rarity in our day and age. Many times, people give with the hopes that they will get something more in return. However, we don't see that type of mentality within the New Testament. We see people who realized that their stuff, their entertainment, their earthly pleasures, were less important than the money that was needed in order for the mission of God to continue advancing.

We also see within the New Testament that a new giving standard was being created by the early disciples. The concept of tithing (giving 10% back to God) is not really found in the New Testament. To be sure, NT people were encouraged to give at least a tenth of their income back to God, but they were also encouraged to give all-they-could.

In the 18th century, John Wesley, a movement-maker, is famous for saying to his bands of Christ followers, "Make all you can, save all you can, and give all you can!" Wesley not only encouraged his bands to give everything they could to the mission, but he also modeled this type of sacrificial giving. As Wesley's income increased, he kept his living expenses the same and increased his giving even more. In his regenerated heart, he wasn't okay with making 80k and only tithing 8k to the mission of God.

Wesley was truly focused on the eternal reward.

I recently read about a pastor who was being convicted about his giving priorities. He felt compelled to give more to the work of the Lord. He and his wife sat down, looked at their finances, and made a commitment in their heart that the biggest check that they would write would be to their local church community. After their initial financial review, they discovered that their largest payment was their house payment. So, they decided to write a monthly check which topped their house payment. They are now discovering the immense joy that sacrificial giving has caused in their life.

I also heard about another network of people who have decided to live below the median income within their area. They got online, found out what the median income was in their area, and whatever income they made above and beyond that level, they decided to give to their church community regardless of the percentage. Many of them are giving up to 50% of their income away to the mission of God.

This movement toward the median reminds me of the story of Zacchaeus (the wee little manipulative tax collector). Zac climbed up a sycamore tree to see what he could see. Jesus took note of Zac's interest and said, "Zac, I'm coming to your house for dinner tonight." After Jesus interacted with Zac that evening, Zac's heart was so stirred that he stood up and said to the Lord, "Look, half of my possessions, I will give to the poor, and if I have defrauded anyone of anything, I will pay them back four times as much." Then Jesus said to him, "Today, salvation has come to this house, because he too is a son of Abraham. For the Son of Man came to seek out and to save the lost."[28]

The story of Zacchaeus is striking. Here we see a self-centered thief encounter Jesus, experience salvation, and the *first* thing he decided to do was to give generously and sacrificially.

This desire to give as a result of experiencing the gift of salvation is not uncommon throughout the Scriptures. In the third chapter of Luke, we see John the Baptist calling people to repentance and paving the way for the Messiah. After John presented his repentance message someone from the crowd asked him, "So, what should we do then?"[29]

John answered, "Anyone who has two shirts should share with the one who has none, and anyone who has food should do the same."[30]

A few moments later, some tax collectors came to be baptized and they asked John, "What should we do?"

John answered, "Don't collect any more than you are required to."[31]

Then some soldiers asked him, "And what should we do?"

John replied, "Don't extort money, don't accuse people falsely, and be content with your pay."

Do you see the common thread throughout all of John's responses?

Each response to the question, "What should we do after we repent?" has to deal with money.

One might think that the first thing a person ought to do after they repent is to begin praying, start studying the Scriptures, or engage in the rituals of the local synagogue. But John's prophetic vision doesn't begin with any of those things. John begins with a prophetic vision of sharing, giving generously, not stealing from others, and being content with one's pay.

Imagine that.

After John's repentance teaching, I think it is safe to say that the movement of God is a movement of people who have reordered their finances according to God's standards and are willing to give generously and sacrificially into God's mission in the world. Similar to how God was able to re-use Zacchaeus after his conversion, God desires to do the same with every one of His followers. God doesn't need our money, but He does need our fully engaged hearts. When we give to God's mission in the world, we're giving God our hearts.

And got wants *all* of our heart.

Nothing less.

By all earthly standards most of the pastors within our network of churches do not live on very much money and I suspect that everyone is struggling to make ends meet.

Our network churches are always living in the tension of wondering if we are going to make it and questioning whether or not if the funds will be there to continue the mission. I'll be the first to admit, it's not an easy tension to live within. Nevertheless, we are putting our trust in the Lord and believe that God will fuel His movement.

It's not very often that you hear people talk about the joy of sacrificial giving, but there are some incredible stories within our network of people who have discovered that sacrificial giving is *the* secret to strengthen their faith.

Sacrificial giving can be likened to working out. If you want to strengthen your muscles, then you must work them beyond their current ability. In other words, you must lift a weight that is heavy enough to exhaust you by lifting it 5-7 times. Lifting a very light weight many times will not strengthen and enlarge your muscles.

One of the reasons I believe God calls us to give sacrificially is that it strengthens our faith and helps us grow spiritually. If we merely give out of our excess we don't give God the opportunity to prove His faithfulness. That's like lifting a very light weight. It won't strengthen our faith muscles. But when we give sacrificially, when we give to the point of it hurting a bit, we exercise our faith.

We learn to trust in God by giving Him a chance to prove Himself trustworthy.

This desire to exercise our faith, even in the midst of financial uncertainty, is at the heart of being a fully devoted follower of Jesus Christ.

Sometimes I find it quite ironic that on every piece of money in America, the same four words are printed: "In God we trust." That phrase might be one of the biggest inconsistencies in the American way. If we're honest, we should probably admit that most of us put a lot more trust in the security of money than we do in the security of God's promises.

In all of our network churches, we are attempting to repaint the American dream. In fact, we are attempting to wipe out the American dream and replace it with God's dream. We teach that when we give it's not for God's benefit and it's not for the church's benefit, it's for our benefit. We need to give generously into God's eternal dream, because when we do, it strengthens our faith and protects us from falling into the facade of the American scream.

One of the most beautiful stories of sacrificial giving arose out of Impact Church in the summer of 2010. Without a doubt, Impact had a financial crisis on their hands, but the real crisis was that they might have been put into a position where they were going to be required to lay off staff and limit their funding for church planting initiatives. The leadership of Impact did not want to sound "needy," but there was certainly a real kingdom need that had to be communicated.

After a gripping teaching series on money, the body of Impact responded with a cry of generosity. People began to see that their money (which is ultimately God's money) really mattered and their giving really affected the movement at large. Bands of people started selling their possessions. Kids were raising change for *change*. And families were restructuring their finances so that they could give more and more.

As a result of this releasing of generosity, God's movement didn't take a step back—it surged forward.

News of this awakening of generosity spread to all the churches in the network and soon many others were rising up in sacrificial giving.

Here are some of the sacrificial things that people did in order to support the mission of God in the land:

One person sold his camper.

Three people sold vehicles.

Two people sold motorcycles.

One individual sold a huge generator.

One woman sold a bunch of gold jewelry.

Several people sold valuable antique furniture.

Many children broke their piggy banks and gave every penny they had.

One couple decided to tithe on their retirement account.

And many other families organized their own movement-minded yard sales.

Through this wave of sacrifice and generosity the local body of Impact was able to raise enough money for their ministry needs, was able to bless the other network churches with several thousand dollars, and gave a gift of $1,000 to the Nazarene church in Lowell. Even more, several network churches began receiving seemingly random checks for 1-2,000 dollars.

The movement of God was moving once again.

And it was all because a few people decided in their hearts to enter into the way of Jesus and live generously and sacrificially.

As the movement of God continues to advance and stretch us financially, our prayer these days is simply this:

> Father, it's so easy to say that we trust in you and in your provision for us and yet we so often find our deepest security in what we own. Help us to distinguish between our wants and our needs. Teach us to simplify the former and trust you for the latter. Set us free from any financial bondage that we may suffer from, that we might be free to give as you graciously provide. Amen.

QUESTIONS TO CONSIDER

1. What is God's perspective on our personal finances? What does God care about most?

2. Does God need our money for His eternal purposes, or not?

3. What is the difference between giving to God out of our abundance and leftovers versus giving to God out of an act of obedience and worship?

4. What do you think about Wesley's statement, "Make all you can, save all you can, and give all you can!"?

5. If you had responded to John the Baptist's repentance message, were baptized, and asked John the question, "What should we do now?" What would John say to you?

STAGE 6
TOWARD LOCAL CONNECTIONS

"Many of us wish we had an apostle Paul to travel with, not realizing how much the leader also needs the close follower."
(Jim Wilson)

"Then the apostles and elders, with the whole church, decided to choose some of their own men and send them to Antioch with Paul and Barnabas. They chose Judas and Silas, men who were leaders among the believers."
(Acts 15:22)

Recently, as I was preparing to move, I realized that after six years of living in my house, I never hung out or sat on my front porch.

In the 1800s the front porch was beginning to gain popularity in the housing industry. By the late nineteenth and early twentieth centuries, front-wrap-around-porches had become quite distinctive and a central architectural feature to most American homes.

By the 1840s, technology and industrialization had created a substantial leisure class, free from the endless survival chores of the Colonial era. With this free time and new leisure class, came the necessity for people to enjoy this free time. The front porch was an obvious choice, and further elements of leisure, including rocking chairs and wicker furniture also grew in popularity. For the most part, front porch people were locally connected and always willing to wave and have a conversation.

However, in the 1960s and 70s, social desires began to change and so did front porches. Home builders were beginning to receive requests to build elaborate back porches. The back porch movement was unstoppable. People wanted to privatize their lives. Now, for the most part, people like me no longer even use their front porches.

When we moved into our house six years ago, I had the vision that our neighbors would all come over, help us move in, and bring us a homemade cherry pie (with the laces and ice cream on top).

Boy was I wrong.

We quickly discovered that if we were going to get to know our neighbors, then we were going to have to initiate the relationship.

Culture certainly has changed. Broadly speaking, people used to be more connected with one another, but now the society has become pretty reserved, standoffish and phone-focused. No longer do relational connections just happen naturally. We must take the first step.

As followers of Jesus, we know that the primary way the good news of Jesus spreads is through relationships. People need our elbow nudges. However, developing relationships is no longer an easy task.

In our network churches, we have discovered that if we want our churches to change the world, then we must start in our own backyards.

Recently, Jim Bowen moved into Westland, MI, in order to start a new missional outpost. Jim and his family have essentially parachuted into Westland. They do not have any preexisting relationships, and besides a District leadership team, nobody has asked them to plant a new church in their community. Jim is simply a radical follower of Jesus and he trusts that, over time, the relationships he builds with people around him will lead to a new body of believers.

Recently, Jim hosted a grill-out with several of his new friends and a few people that he was introduced to through his son's football league. Jim understands that movement outward begins with him.

Jim is an incredible model for what it means to be locally connected and, as it is with all of our network leaders, Jim really wants to see the church expand in his own backyard.

I'm sure there are many stories in the world of church people who do not come across very neighborly. I once heard a story about a church community that had a backyard neighbor ask to borrow the church's tractor in order to remove a tree which had partially fallen onto the bordering fence. The neighbor asked the church maintenance man if he could use the church tractor to remove the tree. And apparently, the maintenance man replied, "I'm sorry; our tractor can only be used for church things on church property."

I'm pretty sure I know what that neighbor was thinking after he heard that response!

Imagine with me if this particular church had taken a different disposition with their property and communal assets. What if the church had sent out a flyer to all of their neighbors and said, "Hi there, our church just got a new tractor, and we just wanted to let you know, if you ever need to borrow it, you certainly could. We'll even send someone over to operate it for you."

Now that would be a different story!

In our network churches, we try to emphasize the fact that all of our communal and personal property, including our tractors, should be used as tools to show people Jesus.

We believe that the job of the church is to hold up or carry Jesus, the Light, into the dark and confused world. Jesus is the hope of the world and the job of the church is to hold up that very hope.

In Revelation 1:10-12, there is an incredibly important image which captures this holding-up-Jesus theology.

John says,

> I was in the Spirit on the Lord's Day, and I heard behind me a loud voice like a sound of a trumpet,

> saying, 'Write in a book what you see, and send it to the seven churches: to Ephesus and to Smyrna and to Pergamum and to Thyatira and to Sardis and to Philadelphia and to Laodicea.' And I turned to see the voice that was speaking with me. And having turned, I saw seven golden *lampstands*.

Jesus tells John to write down everything that was being revealed to him and pass it along to seven specific churches within Asia Minor. Throughout Revelation, John used many first century images and symbols to help communicate the message of Jesus.

In chapter one, it becomes clear that the seven golden lampstands are a symbol for the seven churches that John was writing to. The second and third chapters go into greater detail about the successes and failures of these seven churches, and describe many of the characteristics of the lampstands.

Within the lampstand imagery, the first thing we notice is that the churches were visible.

Unfortunately, these days, the word *church* is often used to describe other things than what the lampstands originally symbolized. So often, people use the word *church* to refer to a building which was built for the purpose of worship and Christian education. But the word *church* never meant building or environments in the Bible. God had something completely different in mind when He used the term *church* in the Scripture.

So, the seven golden lampstands do not represent seven buildings, at least not the kind made with brick, wood and stone.

The word *church* refers to a band of visible people who are living in Christ and community.

John also describes the lampstands (the churches) as "golden."

In ancient thought, gold was a symbol of great value and purity. In Jesus' mind, the church was extremely precious (which probably explains why Jesus was so concerned with their faithfulness and fruitfulness).

Even more, John mentions that the churches were *holding up the Light*.

A lampstand supports and allows the lamp to shine further.

In Revelation, Jesus wanted it to be clear that the *church is not* the light of the world. The church is *holding up and supporting* the Light of the world.[32] Sadly, many people have confused the church with Jesus. The goal of launching a new church or even a church planting network is not to get people to connect to the church. The goal of any church ought to be to connect people to Christ—and Christ alone.

We live in an app-saturated world. "There's an app for that," as the saying goes. Although, when it comes to a relationship with God, through Jesus, there are no apps for that. It's not God plus a great church facility. It's not God plus a house. It's not God plus a family. It's not God plus a spouse. It's not God plus a job. And it's not God plus our sense of happiness.

It's just God!

In all of our network churches, we realize that we can't control how people speak about our churches, but we hope that people speak more about their relationship with Christ than they do about their church identity. We hope that they speak more about Christ than they do about their pastoral leaders. We hope that they speak more about the way of Jesus than they do about the programs of the church.

Within the body of Ignite, there is a special story that fills Jim Nora's heart with immense joy. A gentleman named Bob, who is in his mid 60s, came into Ignite one day and introduced himself to Jim with this statement: "I have been in and out of churches my entire life. Four weeks is the maximum amount of time that I've stayed in one church. I wanted to introduce myself because I probably won't be around in a few weeks and I didn't want you to wonder why I was missing. I simply can't stand church politics and church leadership, and there is always something that rubs me the wrong way."

That might be one of the strangest introductions, but we are happy to acknowledge that this statement was made about a year and a half ago. Bob is still a part of Ignite. In fact, Bob is now a co-leader of the prayer ministry and he is actively leading a group of men who are struggling with addictions.

The reason Bob remained committed was not Ignite's flashy programs or events, but because he saw the living Christ in the body of Ignite and he loves it.

Within the body of Ignite, there is also a girl named Polly, who was a former priestess in the Wiccan cult. A few years ago, Polly was exposed to the ministry of Impact. She connected at Impact the first time only to hear a friend of hers sing in the worship band (this was shortly after a very difficult divorce). Polly didn't know what to expect, but she did encounter the living Jesus. Polly was baptized, but there were still many remnants of Wiccan paraphernalia around her house. Once Polly heard that the body of Ignite was forming, God began to draw Polly back to Himself. Polly is a firefighter. So the name of Ignite caught her attention. Polly became a regular Igniter, but people around her quickly discovered that she was leading a double life. One day, Jim boldly said to Polly, "You either cleanse your home of all your witchcraft paraphernalia or you quit connecting into Ignite!"

Needless to say, Jim's aggressive approach caught Polly's attention, and she agreed to let her old life go. Jim and a few other individuals went to her house to identify all the items of the Wiccan lifestyle in her home. Shortly after, a number of people from Ignite took all of Polly's Wiccan items and burned them in a bonfire. During the cleansing, Jim took notice that Polly was actually having physical reactions as they removed her idols. The night after the bonfire Jim and a group of others prayed over Polly to be cleansed of all Wiccan influences. During the prayer time,

Polly suffered severe chest pains and was driven to the hospital by ambulance. She was released that night with no medical reason for her pain.

Light was pushing out the dark—literally.

Nowadays, Polly is serving God with all her heart, soul, mind and strength. Recently, she publicly rededicated her life to Jesus. Polly is also answering God's call on her life and has enrolled into a Chaplain program in hopes to carry Jesus' light to others who find themselves in darkness.

The story of Polly is a glaring reminder that the work of the church is not to be the hope, but to lift up the Hope. The only one who can push out the darkness is Jesus the Christ.

You see, at the end of the day, the attraction of our churches is not our facility, props on the stage, the band or the humorous speaker.

The attraction of our churches is Christ the Lord. Remember, Jesus said, "*I* am the Light of the world."[33]

As a child, I was taught the song, "This little light of mine, I'm going to let it shine. This little light of mine, I'm going to let it shine. Let it shine. Let it shine. Let it shine..."

People need the Light. And it's our job to connect with them.

Let's just say, our back porches are sacred ground.

QUESTIONS TO CONSIDER

1. How has the society or culture affected how relationships are developed?
2. Who did God use in your life to draw you into His kingdom? How did God use this person?
3. In what ways do you or your church community hold-up-Jesus?
4. When was the last time you saw light pushing out the dark in your church community?
5. In what ways might you be able to emphasize Jesus Christ more than the dynamics of your church community?

STAGE 7
TOWARD GLOBAL ACTIVITY

"When we reflect on the history of the Church, are we not bound to confess that she has failed to follow the example of her Founder? All too often she has worn the robes of the ruler, not the apron of the servant."
(Michael Green)

"But you will receive power when the Holy Spirit comes on you; and you will be my witnesses in Jerusalem, and in all Judea and Samaria, and to the ends of the earth."
(Acts 1:8)

Jesus was pretty clear about where he wanted the kingdom of God to go.

In Jesus' final address he said to his disciples, "Therefore go and make disciples of *all nations*, baptizing them in the name of the Father and of the Son and of the Holy Spirit, and teaching them to obey everything I have commanded you. And surely I am with you always, to the very end of the age."

The key word here is *all*.

Because of our hope-filled theology, we are convinced and convicted that the entire world is our responsibility. We may not be able to do all things for all people all at once, but we can and should be doing something.

Each of our network churches contains a global component; however, we also have a global network aspect too.

The *Nitrogen Network* knows no geographical boundaries.

Collectively, we have sent out two residential church planters across the globe. We have been able to do this type of global work primarily because each network church contributes a tenth of their funds into a collective planting fund. Out of this fund, we have been able to support our European mission leaders, Dennis and Gwen Jackson.

Dennis has been a leader in the church for decades. He is an excellent voice of wisdom; however, some people would say he is simply crazy. A few years ago, Dennis had reached a point in his ministry where he could have easily coasted until retirement. Dennis led a growing church in Michigan, but his heart had become strangely burdened for the European continent. Europe was once a catalytic region of the church, but in the past few decades, the church in Europe has almost become non-existent.

Dennis could have done a lot of easier things in ministry; however, he decided to follow the Spirit's promptings into Europe and launch a new regional strategy for evangelistic prayer and church planting.

Just recently we caught word about a church in Poland led by native Piotr and Joanna Gasiorowski, two of Dennis' leaders. Piotr is leading a new church in Krakow, which is already known for reaching the next generation. The community that Piotr is ministering in could be described as thoroughly religious, yet missing Christ. Many people are responding to the message of moving beyond religion and into a relationship with Christ. The government of Poland has invited Piotr to train its leaders which will hopefully open up more doors of opportunity.

The *Nitrogen Network* has a unique connection with Dennis and we feel privileged to assist in his global ministry.

In addition to Dennis, the *Nitrogen Network* is also coming around Josh, and his wife, Leslie, who were the former student ministry leaders at Impact. Josh felt a burden for the people of another country and is currently making plans to move.

(Because this country is closed to the public expression of the gospel and church, I will keep Josh's last name and the name of the country secret).

Josh is passionate about taking the message of Jesus into places that have no exposure to the good news. Sometimes, those of us in America can become numb to the reality that there are still areas in the world where people do not have churches on every corner and they are not free to worship Christ our Lord. Josh loves to take the horse-blinders off of Americans and help them see that there is a world where people think of Jesus as the guy down the street, not the Master of all creation.

Josh is currently in the process of raising funds in order to make the global move. However, there is no doubt in anyone's minds that once he arrives, a burst of good news will too.

We also have another unique connection to a church planting network and movement in Panama. A gentleman from Epic named Chris Brace made the initial connection with our Panamanian friends. Many other church plants have partnered with a sister church plant in Panama. The country of Panama is peppered with a lot of religiosity, but this particular church planting network (led by Jose McKella) is bringing the real Jesus to real people.

The Panamanian natives are known as the Kuna Indians. The Kunas are a wonderful people group but, by and large, they have not been exposed to the way of Jesus. Our connection with Jose is very unique and their church planters are teaching us a thing or two about maintaining a passion for Christ in a culture filled with resistance.

To be sure, the *Nitrogen Network* thinks glocally.

We take Jesus seriously when he said to go into *all* of the nations.

Some might say it's naive, but we really do believe in the reality that every man, woman and child in the world should have the opportunity to see the living Jesus.

And in order for that dream to come true we pray for revival in the land.

Throughout history, there have been many spiritual awakenings which have recaptured individuals and nations. One reawakening movement that we like to look back on is the Welsh Revival of the early 1900s.

The revival in the rolling hills of Wales brought an extra 100,000 converts according to the estimates of the time and a movement that quickly spread to the four corners of the world. The uniqueness of the Welsh Revival was that it had a very small and humble beginning.

Florrie Evans

This particular movement of the Spirit didn't begin with the great preachers of the day, but instead included, young teenage girls, such as Florrie Evans, from New Quay, Cardigan. In February of 1904, Florrie was in a youth meeting and declared publicly that she loved the Lord Jesus with all of her heart. With these words the Spirit seemed to fall on the meeting and the fire quickly spread to other young people in the Cardiganshire area.

In September of the same year, an Evangelist named Seth Joshua was addressing a convention which included several young people at Blaenanerch just five miles north of Cardigan. Seth himself had been praying for years that God would raise up a young person from the pits to revive the churches.

Seth Joshua

Little did he know that on Thursday, September 29, 1904 his prayer was to be answered in a life changing experience for one 26 year old student, Evan Roberts.

Evan Roberts was born in 1878 in the small town of Loughor in Glamorgan, just seven miles away from Swansea. For years Evan had been a faithful member of Moriah Calvinistic Methodist Church at Loughor. He was a Sunday School leader, a conscientious reader of the main theological works of his day and, more than that, he had been praying for revival to break out for over 11 years.

Evan Roberts

Having been converted as a young teenager, he continued to pray regularly that God would again visit the nation of Wales in a powerful manner. *Determined to do his part*, he felt compelled to pursue a formal theological education. It was only two and a half weeks after he arrived at college that he found himself at a crossroads in his spiritual experience.

A spiritual experience which would lead him back to the young people of his own church where he would share his story and encourage them to be open to the promptings of God.

Within two weeks, the Welsh Revival was national news and before long, Evan Roberts, his brother Dan and his best friend Sidney were traveling the country conducting revival meetings. However, these meetings were different than the typical revival meetings of the past. Often the ministers just sat down unable to preach or even understand what kind of faith-winds had blown through their usually sedate church gatherings.

Annie Davies

This was a revival with youth on fire—both men and women. After the first stirrings amongst the young women of New Quay, young women continued to play an important part in the revival work. Young Florrie went on a team to North Wales with her friend Maud and used their voices as instruments of God's message. Amongst the most well known was Annie Davies Maesteg who accompanied Evan Roberts on his missions.

Yes a great wind had hit the churches yet for so many it was a wind of love and power which completely transformed their lives.

People were changed in so many ways. The crime rate dropped, drunkards were reformed, pubs reported losses in trade. Bad language disappeared and never returned to the lips of many. It was reported that the pit ponies failed to understand their born again coal miners who seemed to speak the new language of God—without curse, negativity and blasphemy. Even football and rugby became uninteresting in the light of new joy and direction received by the converts. Coal miners and tin-men of the working classes expressed their joy in many ways. But perhaps the song that captured what most of these converts felt was a song sung by Sam Jenkins, a tin plate worker from Llanelli. The song was called *Am Achub hen rebel fel fi*, which in English means, "For saving an old rebel like me."

The revival winds that had blown through the hills and valleys of Wales in the dying months of 1904 soon became a movement that affected the world. Visitors from France, Turkey, the U.S., India and other countries, came to Wales. They caught the flame and passed it on to new countries. Welsh communities throughout the world felt the effects of God's powerful work, and soon had many other churches praying that God would visit them as well.

The public excitement of the revival had died down by 1906. Evan Roberts went to Leicester to recuperate. The newspapers went back to politics and other things, but for many, the honeymoon of these two years developed into a lasting and loving relationship with a risen Christ that continued a lifetime.

When one elderly revival convert was asked as to whether the revival stopped in 1906, she answered, "It's still burning within my heart. It's never been extinguished. It has burned for over 70 years."[34]

A hundred years from now, we don't know what people will say or write about the *Nitrogen Network*. We don't want or need any recognition, but in our own heart of hearts, it would be wonderful to know that our seeming small band of Christ followers created a magnificent wave of the Spirit that truly did turn lives toward Christ. Maybe one day a future historian will e-post a cheesy picture of Phil Struckmeyer, Steve Cymbal, Ed Love, Jason Holdridge, Jim Nora, Jim Bowen, Duane Bower, Rob Lawrence, and Josh McCracken, and say of the *Nitrogen Network*, "The third great awakening in the Americas had a very small beginning. A former school teacher named Phil

Struckmeyer felt the Spirit of the living Lord tell him to do his part. As a result, the movement of God spread from the Americas, to Europe and Turkey and Panama and New Zealand and Africa and to many other countries. The revival caused hundreds of thousands to turn away from their old nature and embrace their new nature in Christ Jesus. Without a doubt, the movement of God was and is still alive!"

We don't know what the Spirit of our Lord will do in our land, but we like to imagine the possibilities.

And we only want to do our part.

QUESTIONS TO CONSIDER

1. In what ways can the church become more servant-like in the world?

2. Why did Jesus paint a picture of God's movement always going outward?

3. Why did Jesus want his followers to live with the sense that they were contributing to the kingdom's expansion?

4. How often do you pray for revival in the land?

5. In a hundred years from now, what will people say about your faith and works?

CONCLUSION
TOWARD A NEW WORLD

"Prophets are almost extinct in the religious world today. The modern church is a 'non-prophet' organization."
(Vance Havner)

"The Church which is married to the spirit of its age will be a widow in the next."
(Dean W.R. Inge)

A few months ago, I was informed that Apple's CEO, Steve Jobs (iSteve), resigned from his role.

Recently, I learned that iSteve passed away at the age of 56.

At the time of iSteve's resignation, and again after his death, he was widely described as a visionary, pioneer and genius. Steve was perhaps one of the foremost in the field of business, innovation, product design, and a man who had profoundly changed the face of the modern world. His death was widely mourned and considered a loss to the world by commentators across the globe. Many people have proclaimed that Steve turned the tech world upside down.

One of the core convictions within all of our network churches is that we have one life to live, and we can either live in a standstill or we can *turn* this world around.

In a commencement address at Stanford, Steve Jobs stated, "No one wants to die. Even people who want to go to heaven don't want to die to get there. And yet, death is the destination we all share. No one has ever escaped it, and that is how it should be, because death is very likely the single best invention of life. It's life's change agent. It clears out the old and makes way for the new."

I don't know what Steve thought about Jesus, but Steve's perspective on death was very biblical.

On the top of my dresser I have a fish bowl filled with popcorn kernels. Each kernel represents a week of my life. About four years ago I decided to calculate how many weeks I would live if I was allowed to live until the average male life expectancy rate (which is now 75.6 in the U.S.). Each Saturday, on my day of rest, I take out a kernel, toss it in the trash can and pray Psalm 90:12, "Lord, teach me to number my days so that I may gain a heart of wisdom."

I'm not sure why I chose to use popcorn kernels. My original idea was to use Double-Bubble, but then someone wiser than me mentioned that in 40 years it might be too hard to chew. For me, the counting-of-my-kernels is one of my favorite spiritual disciplines. Each week I am reminded to take nothing for granted and to live each day as if I were a gallon of milk and knew my expiration date.

I have no doubt that all of the leaders within our planting network share this same desire. We want nothing more than to leave this world with a Christ-honoring legacy. We don't just want to be known as good people—we want to be known as gospel people.

You see, we don't just want to make a difference in the world—we want to make a different world.

It's game time—my friends.

And we have a mission to accomplish.

According to Revelation 21, heaven has been brought down to earth. God is with His people, but the dark and despair-filled world still needs help seeing the hope of the Holy City.

That's where we come in.

God has called every one of his children to follow in His footsteps.

And God isn't slowing down due to age.

In fact, God is picking up steam.

Someone once said, "The world is God's treadmill." Even though it's not entirely theologically correct, it's a good way to describe a living and active God. God really is longing for the world to be *turned* around.

In the Greek language there are two primary words used for the word time. *Chronos* is the word which is used for describing sequential time. For instance, when we speak about studying biblical events which happened consecutively in history we use the word *chronology* to describe the order.

The other Greek word for time is the word *Kairos*. *Kairos* means the right or opportune moment. The ancient Greeks referred to *kairos* as “the supreme moment.” *Kairos* signifies a time in between, a moment of indeterminate time in which something special happens. A *kairos* moment could be your salvation, your baptism, or your calling into a missional opportunity.

Typically, *kairos* moments can be recognized because they leave you marked in some way.

Perhaps, after reading this book and hearing about the *Nitrogen Network* stories, the Spirit of our Lord is beginning to stir up a *kairos* moment in you.

Maybe you are beginning to realize that God wants to use you (the good, the bad, and the ugly), to bring the light of Christ to the people around you.

Maybe God has sparked a dormant desire in you to participate in a new church start in your community, or go into another city, or join the *Nitrogen* team, or start a new network of mission-minded churches in your region.

“The *kairos* has come,” Jesus said. “The kingdom of God is near. Repent and believe the good news!” (Mark 1:15)

May the *turning* begin.

ABOUT THE AUTHOR

Dr. Ed Love has catalyzed and cultivated several new church communities. Ed is currently serving as the lead follower and pastor of a new missional outpost called *The Well*. With an immense passion to help people hear and see the living Jesus, Ed spends his time teaching, writing, and discipling others in the Way. Ed holds an MDIV from Asbury Theological Seminary and a DMIN from George Fox Evangelical Seminary. He lives in Ionia, MI with his wife, Emily, and three children, Jennah, Josiah and Micah.

ABOUT PHIL STRUCKMEYER

Phil is from Lowell, MI, where he lives with his wife Andrea and three kids, Drew, Nick and Emily. Phil is currently the Network Pastor of Impact and the Nitrogen Network Catalyst. Impact is the church Phil started in 2003 with the vision of planting three churches in five years and ten in ten. Impact has been the parent and grandparent church of four additional churches and four developing planting projects. Before going into ministry, Phil was a high school biology teacher. Outside of ministry, Phil loves living life to the full with his family and lives to reproduce the life of Jesus in our world.

pstruckmeyer@nitrogennetwork.net
www.nitrogennetwork.net
www.motionminded.blogspot.com

Nitrogen's Mailing Address:
1069 Lincoln Lake / Lowell, MI 49331

THE NITROGEN NETWORK SPECS

Nitrogen is a church planting network mobilizing planters, churches, districts and networks to start church planting movements in North America and beyond.

VISION

What if fresh and forceful expressions of the Church were raised up to re-incarnate a life-changing, world-transforming vision of the Great Commandment?

MISSION

What if a fresh and forceful outbreak of God's redemptive will began to unfold through a radical mobilization of the Great Commission?

VALUES

What if the Church became?

- MOVEMENT-MINDED
- KINGDOM-ORIENTED
- RE-INCARNATED
- REDEMPTIVELY-FOCUSED
- GENEROUSLY-SACRIFICIAL
- LOCALLY-CONNECTED
- GLOBALLY-ACTIVE

STRATEGY

What if God would show us again how to . . .

1. Recruit and mobilize high-capacity planters, leaders and teams

2. Identify highly receptive cities and sites as strategic planting contexts

3. Empower robust resources of prayer, renewal and capital

. . . in order to see the Church rise again in our world?

NITROGEN NARRATIVE IN BRIEF

Nitrogen is a church planting network that has emerged out of Impact Church and the West Michigan District of the Wesleyan Church. Impact is a church plant that launched in the fall of 2003 by an adventurous band of Christ-followers with the purpose and vision of planting three churches in five years and ten in ten. With the birth of Epic, Encounter, Ignite, Pathway (a granddaughter),The Well (a great-granddaughter) and the development of four new multiplication projects, God is doing an incredible work of raising up bands of Christ followers who are raising up bands of Christ-followers.

The West Michigan District has planted 22 churches from 2000-2011 and has truly experienced the infancy of a multiplication movement.

Nitrogen has developed out of the best practices of recruiting, assessing, training, coaching, networking church planters, and has initiated a process of mobilizing key leaders, teams, churches, districts, prayer warriors and finances so that the movement of church multiplication can continue with great enthusiasm.

A SNAPSHOT OF A NITROGEN HUDDLE

FOR MORE NITROGEN INFORMATION OR NEXT STEPS GO TO:

WWW.NITROGENNETWORK.NET

OTHER WORKS BY DR. LOVE

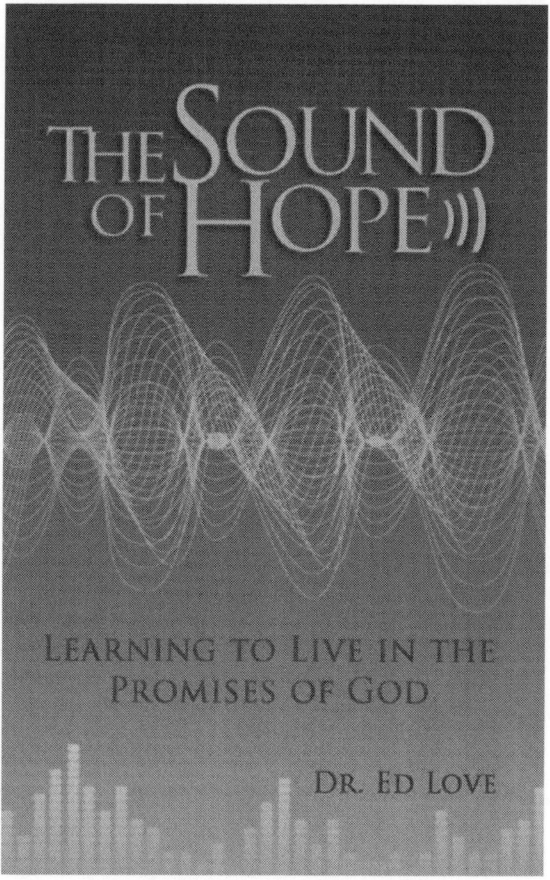

FOR SALE ON AMAZON.COM
VIEW THE BOOK TRAILER AT *THE-SOUND-OF-HOPE.NET*

ENDNOTES

[1] Duin, Julia. *Quitting Church: Why the Faithful are Fleeing and What to Do About It* (Grand Rapids, MI: Baker Books, 2008), 13. Duin sites George Barna's research on the percentage of people who disconnect from the church each year. Duin also notes that Americans are not disinterested in spiritual matters; they are simply not going to church to feed a spiritual interest.

[2] Olson, David. *The American Church in Crisis* (Grand Rapids, MI: Zondervan, 2008), 31.

[3] Ibid.

[4] Ibid.

[5] Ibid.

[6] Sanchez, Daniel. *Church Planting Movements in North America* (Fort Worth, TX: Church Starting Network, 2007), 18. Also see, Hirsch, Allen. *The Forgotten Ways: Reactivating the Missional Church* (Grand Rapids, MI: Brazos Press, 2007), 45.

[7] Barna study group statistic (see www.barna.org).

[8] See Matthew 9:37-38.

[9] Matthew 28:19-20.

[10] Matthew 22:36-40.

[11] 1 Corinthians 1:27.

[12] Barclay, William. *The Gospel of Luke* (Louisville, KY: Westminster John Knox Press, 1975), 120-123.

[13] See 2 Corinthians 12:9.

[14] See 2 Corinthians 12:10.

[15] Matthew 18:19-20.

[16] Barclay, William. *The Gospel of Matthew* (Louisville, KY: Westminster John Knox Press, 1975), 191.

[17] See Matthew 5:17.

[18] See Galatians 6:9.

[19] See Matthew 5:16.

[20] See Matthew 13:24-29.

[21] See Matthew 13: 37-43.

[22] Wikipedia contributors. "How Great Thou Art (hymn)." Wikipedia, The Free Encyclopedia. (Accessed on 4 Dec. 2011).

[23] Matthew 20:26-28.

[24] See Luke 16:10.

[25] Philippians 2:5-11.

[26] See Matthew 6:9-13.

[27] Matthew 6:21.

[28] Luke 19: 8-10 (NRSV).

[29] Luke 3:10.

[30] Luke 3:11.

[31] Luke 3:13.

[32] See John 3:19-21; 8:12.

[33] See John 9:5.

[34] Wikipedia contributors. "1904–1905 Welsh Revival." Wikipedia, The Free Encyclopedia. (Accessed on 21 Nov. 2011).

11165602R00077

Made in the USA
Charleston, SC
03 February 2012